3/13

DATE DUE

APR 2 9 2013	
MAY 2 3 2013	

DISCARDED

EYE ON
Art

COMIC ART

by Michael V. Uschan

LUCENT BOOKS
A part of Gale, Cengage Learning

GALE
CENGAGE Learning·

Detroit • New York • San Francisco • New Haven, Conn • Waterville, Maine • London

LIBRARY OF CONGRESS CATALOGING-IN-PUBLICATION DATA

Uschan, Michael V., 1948-
  Comic art / by Michael V. Uschan.
     p. cm. -- (Eye on art)
  Summary: "These books provide a historical overview of the development of different types of art and artistic movements; explore the roots and influences of the genre; discuss the pioneers of the art and consider the changes the genre has undergone"-- Provided by publisher.
  Includes bibliographical references and index.
  ISBN 978-1-4205-0862-8 (hardback)
  1. Comic books, strips, etc.--History and criticism--Juvenile literature.
  I. Title.
  NC1355.U83 2012
  741.5'9--dc23
                                                         2012022249

Lucent Books
27500 Drake Rd.
Farmington Hills, MI 48331

ISBN-13: 978-1-4205-0862-8
ISBN-10: 1-4205-0862-8

Printed in the United States of America
1 2 3 4 5 6 7 16 15 14 13 12

CONTENTS

Foreword

"Art has no other purpose than to brush aside . . . everything that veils reality from us in order to bring us face to face with reality itself."

—French philosopher Henri-Louis Bergson

Some thirty-one thousand years ago, early humans painted strikingly sophisticated images of horses, bison, rhinoceroses, bears, and other animals on the walls of a cave in southern France. The meaning of these elaborate pictures is unknown, although some experts speculate that they held ceremonial significance. Regardless of their intended purpose, the Chauvet-Pont-d'Arc cave paintings represent some of the first known expressions of the artistic impulse.

From the Paleolithic era to the present day, human beings have continued to create works of visual art. Artists have developed painting, drawing, sculpture, engraving, and many other techniques to produce visual representations of landscapes, the human form, religious and historical events, and countless other subjects. The artistic impulse also finds expression in glass, jewelry, and new forms inspired by new technology. Indeed, judging by humanity's prolific artistic output throughout history, one must conclude that the compulsion to produce art is an inherent aspect of being human, and the results are among humanity's greatest cultural achievements: masterpieces such as the architectural marvels of ancient Greece, Michelangelo's perfectly rendered statue *David*, Vincent van Gogh's visionary painting *Starry Night*, and endless other treasures.

The creative impulse serves many purposes for society. At its most basic level, art is a form of entertainment or the means for a satisfying or pleasant aesthetic experience. But art's true power lies not in its potential to entertain and delight but in its ability to enlighten, to reveal the truth, and by doing so to uplift the human spirit and transform the human race.

One of the primary functions of art has been to serve religion. For most of Western history, for example, artists were paid by the church to produce works with religious themes and subjects. Art was thus a tool to help human beings transcend mundane, secular reality and achieve spiritual enlightenment. One of the best-known, and largest-scale, examples of Christian religious art is the Sistine Chapel in the Vatican in Rome. In 1508 Pope Julius II commissioned Italian Renaissance artist Michelangelo to paint the chapel's vaulted ceiling, an area of 640 square yards (535 sq. m). Michelangelo spent four years on scaffolding, his neck craned, creating a panoramic fresco of some three hundred human figures. His paintings depict Old Testament prophets and heroes, sibyls of Greek mythology, and nine scenes from the book of Genesis, including the Creation of Adam, the Fall of Adam and Eve from the Garden of Eden, and the Flood. The ceiling of the Sistine Chapel is considered one of the greatest works of Western art and has inspired the awe of countless Christian pilgrims and other religious seekers. As eighteenth-century German poet and author Johann Wolfgang von Goethe wrote, "Until you have seen this Sistine Chapel, you can have no adequate conception of what man is capable of."

In addition to inspiring religious fervor, art can serve as a force for social change. Artists are among the visionaries of any culture. As such, they often perceive injustice and wrongdoing and confront others by reflecting what they see in their work. One classic example of art as social commentary was created in May 1937, during the brutal Spanish civil war. On May 1 Spanish artist Pablo Picasso learned of the recent attack on the small Basque village of Guernica by German airplanes allied with fascist forces led by Francisco Franco. The German pilots had used the village for target practice, a three-hour bombing that killed sixteen hundred civilians. Picasso, living in Paris, channeled his outrage over the massacre into his painting *Guernica*, a black, white, and gray mural that depicts dismembered animals and fractured human figures whose faces are contorted in agonized expressions. Initially, critics and the public condemned the painting as an incoherent hodgepodge, but the work soon came to be seen as a powerful antiwar statement and remains an iconic symbol of the violence and terror that dominated world events during the remainder of the twentieth century.

The impulse to create art—whether painting animals with crude pigments on a cave wall, sculpting a human form from marble, or commemorating human tragedy in a mural—thus serves many purposes. It offers an entertaining diversion, nourishes the imagination and the spirit, decorates and beautifies the world, and chronicles the age. But underlying all these functions is the desire to reveal that which is obscure—to illuminate, clarify, and perhaps ennoble. As Picasso himself stated, "The purpose of art is washing the dust of daily life off our souls."

The Eye on Art series is intended to assist readers in understanding the various roles of art in society. Each volume offers an in-depth exploration of a major artistic movement, medium, figure, or profession. All books in the series are beautifully illustrated with full-color photographs and diagrams. Riveting narrative, clear technical explanation, informative sidebars, fully documented quotes, a bibliography, and a thorough index all provide excellent starting points for research and discussion. With these features, the Eye on Art series is a useful introduction to the world of art—a world that can offer both insight and inspiration.

Introduction

A Powerful New Art Form

In the 1940s, when Will Eisner was stretching the artistic boundaries of comic books with his comic about masked crime fighter the Spirit, he was angry that no one considered the stories he created and the figures he drew to be art. The first comic books were published in the mid-1930s, only three decades after the first comic strips began appearing in newspapers. Comic strips in their infancy were designed for one purpose—to make people laugh—and were referred to variously as "the funnies," "the jokes," and "the comics." Even though new comic strips in the 1930s like *Terry and the Pirates* and *Prince Valiant* were beginning to have complex stories and more refined art, few people believed comic strips had any artistic merit. Comic books had more intricate stories and detailed drawing than comic strips, and artists like Eisner were continuing to develop creative layouts and graphics to make them even more visually exciting. But because people tended to view comic books the same way they did comic strips, Eisner says they failed to win any respect as art. "Comics before that were pretty pictures in sequence, and I was trying to create a new thing, an art form," he explains. "[Instead] I was [viewed as] a comic-book cartoonist and nothing more, laboring in what would soon become a kind of artistic ghetto in which people with authentic, if offbeat, talents had to suffer the disdain of the mainstream."[1]

The lack of respect the art world had for comic art did not begin to fade until the last few decades of the twentieth century. Comic art is a generic term for cartoons, comic strips, and comic books. Cartoons are one-panel comic art, comic strips have multiple panels, comic books have multiple pages, and graphic novels are longer than comic books. The reason for comic art's new stature was the advent of graphic novels that often dealt with serious subjects and had more sophisticated artwork and page layouts. An example is Art Spiegelman's *Maus: A Survivor's Tale*, which is about the Holocaust and in 1991 won a Pulitzer Prize for literature. One reason comic art failed to be recognized as true art for so long was that much of it was geared toward younger readers for entertainment, although many adults also enjoyed it. People tended to think of comics as frivolous, with no artistic merit. However, comic artists have argued that the main reason for the lack of respect for their work was that most people did not understand what comic art was and how hard it was to do it well.

Words and Images

Throughout the ages, people have admired artists who created works of beauty or importance in genres like literature, film, painting, and other visual arts. Comic art historian Robert C. Harvey believes many people failed to consider comic art as art because they were judging it on either its visual or its literary merits and did not understand that it is different from both illustration and literature. Harvey writes that "[comic art is] a hybrid form: words and pictures."[2] He argues that because comic art combines elements of the two older arts to tell stories, make people laugh, or comment on social or political issues, people who claim it is inferior to drawn or written works are judging it by the wrong aesthetic guidelines.

The Smithsonian Institution in Washington, D.C., is the world's largest museum and research complex. In a Smithsonian collection of comic strips that they selected and commented on, editors Bill Blackbeard and Martin Williams hail comic strips as an important American cultural accomplishment. They also claim that comic strips have too often been misjudged for either poor drawing or a weak story. They write that the only true way to judge comic art is to consider the merits of both the drawings and words it comprises:

> A well-conceived story, character, or incident can make clumsy or barely competent art work functionally acceptable. [Indeed] some strip artists were, by strict standards of draftsmanship or graphics, no artist at all. What they had was a point of view (a sometimes rowdy point of view, to be sure) on the human animal and his attitudes and actions, and a functional means to convey it.[3]

Actually, one could argue that any form of comic art should be judged on how well artists have meshed the two arts of illustration and literature into a coherent new form of art. Comic book artist Frank Miller has been praised for his artistic renderings of *Batman* and *Wolverine*, two of the most popular comic book superheroes. In commenting on the artistry of mixing words and pictures in comic art, Miller once said, "The illustrations are not really illustrations of what's going on. The narration isn't really describing what's going on, either. There's a gap there, and somewhere in that gap is reality."[4] What Miller meant was that comic artists use words and pictures to create something greater than the sum of the two individual arts. It is this powerful combination that readers respond to and that raises comic art to the level of art.

Comic art also differs from its two composite arts—drawing and literature—in that it is most often done quickly. Artists who produce daily, weekly, or monthly forms of comic art do not have the luxury to spend as much time creating their work as Leonardo da Vinci did the *Mona Lisa* or J.R.R. Tolkien the *Lord of the Rings* trilogy. Comic art historian Harry Katz explains the predicament artists face while working under the pressure of recurring deadlines:

Cartoonists rarely have time for art for its own sake, which only means that they apply artistry as needed to the task at hand: to convey the message, joke, product, or political opinion. [But] great cartoonists know that humor without art is unlikely to endure, that readers won't linger, and no instant visual connection will be made. They use art . . . [to] create works of lasting beauty.[5]

Despite the time disadvantage they face, comic artists produce works that thrill readers, make them laugh, or do both at the same time. They have also created memorable characters like Popeye, Little Orphan Annie, Superman, and Spider-Man that have become a permanent part of popular culture. And the ability to move people so deeply is one attribute of true art.

Art or Junk?

When Jules Feiffer was only sixteen, he began helping Will Eisner draw *The Spirit*. Feiffer also drew comic strips for four decades and in 1986 won a Pulitzer Prize for editorial cartooning. Despite Feiffer's impressive comic art résumé, he does not care if his work is considered art. In fact, Feiffer considers it junk. He explains, "[Junk] is there to entertain on the basest, most compromised of levels. It finds the lowest common denominator and proceeds from there. [But] readers will say 'I know it's junk, but I like it.' Which is the whole point about junk. It is there to be nothing else but liked. Junk is a second-class citizen of the arts: a status of which we and it are constantly aware."[6]

Whether it is art or junk, many people enjoy comic art. And for Feiffer and other comic artists, that is what really matters.

A History of Comic Art

Scott Adams draws *Dilbert*, a newspaper comic strip that spokes fun at the daily life of office workers. Dilbert is the strip's main character, a geeky engineer who constantly battles his dim-witted boss, who is bald except for two thick wedges of hair that stick up from his head like horns. In the first of three panels in the October 20, 2011, installment of the long-running comic strip, Dilbert's boss tells Dilbert to change the solid lines on plans he had made to dotted lines. His boss explains in the second panel that doing that will save their company money because, "We're not made of ink." But in the final panel Dilbert asks his boss, "Why'd I just get chills?" His boss responds, "Me too. It feels like some sort of forbidden knowledge."[7] The sequence made readers chuckle because Dilbert and his boss are, in fact, made of ink. The two characters owe their existence to the ink that allows the comic strip to be printed.

Although comic strips like *Dilbert* also have an electronic life today on the Internet, most people still read them in newspapers. *Dilbert* is an example of comic art. This is how Robert C. Harvey defines the term: "[Comic art] consists of pictorial narratives or expositions in which words (often lettered into the picture area with speech balloons) usually contribute to the meaning of the picture and vice versa. . . . A pictorial narrative [usually] uses a sequence of pictures [or it] may not as in single-panel cartoons—political cartoons as well as magazine-type cartoons."[8]

Comic art encompasses cartoons, comic strips, comic books, and graphic novels that can be as thick as a book. The popular term for comic art is *comics*, because so much of comic art is designed to amuse people. But comic artists also use their skills to tell adventurous stories and comment about serious political and social issues as well as life in general. Most comic art combines words and pictures, but a few cartoonists—another name for comic artists—produce work with no words.

Single-panel cartoons were the first type of comic art to appear and have been making people laugh or think about various subjects for hundreds of years. Newspapers began running single- and multi-panel comic strips in the 1890s. The first comic books were printed in the 1930s, and the first graphic novels were produced in the last few decades of the twentieth century. The roots of comic art, however, extend much further back in the history of humankind.

The Origin of Comic Art

The first people who used drawings to tell stories or leave evidence of their existence lived more than thirty thousand years ago. Primitive people used simple pigments to paint images of animals and events in their daily life, such as hunting. In 1994 hundreds of such simple yet artistic drawings were discovered in the Chauvet-Pont-d'Arc cave in southeastern France; among the animals depicted were rhinoceroses, lions, and a leopard, animals unknown to Europe in modern times. Similar primitive art has been found in other parts of Europe as well as Africa and Australia.

Even though such people had to struggle daily just to survive, they took time from their harsh, danger-filled lives to create such images. The most common explanation of the motivation of these ancient artists is that they wanted to tell stories about important events in their lives or create sacred

A prehistoric cave painting discovered in France is evidence that humans have been using drawings to tell stories for thousands of years.

images central to their religious beliefs. Drawing those images was the only way people could leave a lasting statement about their lives until written languages were developed about six thousand years ago. But even after writing made it easier for people to express themselves, drawn art continued to play an important role in how people communicated their thoughts, feelings, and beliefs to each other. In fact, as time went by, people discovered that combining words with drawings could make their messages even more powerful, as well as easier to understand. Thus was created comic art, a fusion of two much older art forms—illustration (drawings) and literature (words).

Comic art did not become popular until a few hundred years ago when literacy became widespread so that many people could enjoy it. Once comic art appeared, it quickly became one of the world's most popular arts as well as one of the most beloved types of mass entertainment. Legendary comic artist Will Eisner believes the same human trait that led primitive people to create cave paintings motivates comic artists today. "The telling of a story lies deep in the social behavior of human groups—ancient and modern," Eisner writes. "Stories are used to teach behavior within the community, to discuss morals or values, or to satisfy curiosity. They dramatize social relations and the problems of living, convey ideas or act out fantasies."[9]

Eisner first became prominent in the 1940s with *The Spirit*, his comic book about a mysterious, often humorous masked crime fighter. In 1978 Eisner also helped pioneer the new genre of graphic novels with *A Contract with God, and Other Tenement Stories*. However, the art Eisner helped develop had already been entertaining and educating people for centuries in the form of cartoons.

Cartoons and Caricatures

The word *cartoon* is derived from the Italian word *cartone*, a name for a type of heavy paper on which cartoons were usually drawn. Cartoons are one-panel drawings, usually with words that add meaning to the scene depicted. Cartoons did not become common until after the printing press was invented in the fifteenth century, which allowed them to be widely distributed in newspapers, magazines, and books. This period also saw the beginning of caricature, a type of cartoon that exaggerates someone's physical appearance and depicts the person in ways that mock his or her ideas, personality, or accomplishments. Caricature continues to be a major element today in editorial cartoons, drawings that express opinions about political figures and other issues.

Some of the first great editorial cartoonists were famous European artists who wanted to comment on important political and social issues of the day. Their works were often as skillfully and powerfully drawn as any paintings. In addition to appearing in publications, they were produced as high-quality prints, many of which can be viewed today in museums around the world.

William Hogarth was an acclaimed eighteenth-century English painter who also created cartoons criticizing English life. In 1751 Hogarth produced *Beer Street* and *Gin Lane*, a pair of cartoons on the evils of drinking alcohol. The artistic drawings satirized the increase in alcoholism in England due to the rising consumption of gin, which had become popular because it was cheaper than beer and made people drunk more quickly due to its higher alcohol content. Hogarth's beer drinkers appear happy and prosperous. His gin drinkers look poor, fight with each other, and include a drunken mother who lets her child fall off her lap. Another Hogarth cartoon, titled *The Sleeping Congregation*, shows people sleeping in church during a sermon. Cartoon historian Syd Hoff writes, "Hogarth does not make it clear whether he is satirizing a dull sermon or an indifferent congregation forced to attend church by the social and religious pressures of the time."[10]

Honoré Daumier, a nineteenth-century French painter and sculptor, also used cartoons to criticize social and political issues. In 1831 his *Gargantua* whimsically portrayed French king Louis Philippe as a gruesome giant gorging on taxes fed to him by French citizens. Daumier was sentenced to six months in prison for creating such a brutal caricature of the king. About the same time, famed Spanish painter Francisco Goya created a series of cartoons titled *The Disasters of War* that portrayed the brutality of armed conflict.

English settlers brought cartooning to North America during the seventeenth century, when they began colonizing the land that would become the United States. On May 9, 1754, the first American editorial cartoon appeared in Benjamin Franklin's *Pennsylvania Gazette*. Franklin's drawing of a snake cut into eight sections represented various English colonies or regions; beneath the dissected snake were the words "Join, or Die."[11] The cartoon was Franklin's powerful appeal to colonists to band together to fight the French and their Native American allies in the French and Indian War. The colonists heeded Franklin's advice and won the war. Franklin's cartoon was resurrected during the Revolutionary War to unite the colonies against Great Britain in the war that led to U.S. independence.

JOIN, or DIE.

Editorial cartoons were the main form of comic art in the United States until the 1870s, when magazines like *Puck*, *Judge*, and *Life* began featuring humorous cartoons. Most of these cartoons involved simple-minded puns, like one that shows a golfer in winter preparing to hit a golf ball off a tee over a frozen lake. The caption below the art reads, "Iced Tee,"[12] a pun on "iced tea." Comic historian Stephen Becker writes that most early American cartoons were not very funny: "Collections of wit and humor prior to the First World War show clearly that draftsmanship had outstripped wit. [Few] combine the visual with the verbal to make a cartoon that we can still laugh at [today]. The drawing was good, though."[13]

Among these early comic artists, Hogarth was one of the earliest and also one of the most influential in developing comic art. In addition to being a master cartoonist, Hogarth is credited with being the world's first sequential artist.

Benjamin Franklin appealed to the colonies to band together in 1754 with his "JOIN, or DIE" drawing, which was the first American editorial cartoon.

Sequential Art

The term *sequential art* was first used in 1985 by Will Eisner in *Comics and Sequential Art*, a book that grew out of essays on comic art he wrote while teaching at the School of Visual Arts in New York. Eisner defines sequential art as "a means of creative expression, a distinct discipline, an art and literary form that deals with the arrangement of pictures or images and words to narrate a story or dramatize an idea."[14]

Hogarth sometimes created a series of cartoons on the same topic. Industry and Idleness was a series of twelve cartoons in 1747 that showed differences in the lives of two apprentices; one was a dedicated worker who became rich, while the other was lazy and immoral and ended up being executed as a criminal. The cartoons were Hogarth's way of criticizing what he believed was the poor work ethic of English workers. Each individual cartoon detailed one aspect of the lives of the apprentices, but

A cartoon from William Hogarth's twelve-part Industry and Idleness series shows an apprentice playing a game in a churchyard. The series depicted the poor work ethic of English workers.

when read together as a whole, they combined to tell a more comprehensive story.

Looking back, comic historians decided that Industry and Idleness and similar works by Hogarth were the first examples of sequential art. Sequential art almost always includes words in the form of dialogue or narrative. Some rare examples of sequential art that employ only drawings are *Henry*, a bald-headed youngster who has rarely spoken a word since his comic strip debuted in 1932, and *The Little King*, mute since he began life in a 1931 *New Yorker* cartoon.

Comic strips, comic books, and graphic novels are all considered sequential art. Comic strips were the first sequential art in the United States. And like cartoons, this format also originated in Europe.

The First Comic Strips

Rodolphe Töpffer, a Swiss cartoonist, and Wilhelm Busch, a German painter, were key comic strip innovators. Töpffer's *The Adventures of Obadiah Oldbuck* was published in the United States in 1842, and Busch's drawings about two mischievous boys named Max and Moritz was published two decades later. These early examples of sequential art were primitive ancestors of today's comic strips. They had multiple panels, combined drawings and words, and had a recurring cast of characters, but unlike modern comic strips, they were not published daily in newspapers accessible to most people but as books. An early American prototype comic strip was the six-panel *Mr. Bowler's Midnight Encounter* by noted cartoonist Frank Bellew, which appeared in 1881 in *St. Nicholas Magazine*.

Comic strip historians, however, claim that the first modern comic strip debuted on February 17, 1895, in the *New York World*. Richard F. Outcault was an illustrator who had been drawing cartoons about the antics of poor street kids for *Truth*, a humor magazine. Outcault also worked as an artist for the *New York World*. The newspaper's publisher, Joseph Pulitzer, saw the cartoons and liked them so much that he reprinted one in the Sunday edition of his paper. A second cartoon followed a month later, and on May 5, 1895, the *New York World*

Max and Moritz cause mischief in a drawing from the 1860s by Wilhelm Busch, who is considered a comic strip innovator.

ran a cartoon in color for the first time. Titled *At the Circus in Hogan's Alley*, the single-panel drawing by Outcault showed raggedly dressed kids juggling balls, jumping through paper hoops, and hanging from a wooden post like gymnasts. In the foreground of that cartoon there was a small child with big ears, a curious smile, and a shaved head wearing a tent-like nightshirt. This strange-looking character would soon become the first comic strip superstar.

On January 5, 1896, the bald-headed urchin's shirt was colored bright yellow, and he became known as the Yellow Kid. The *New York World* began running a *Yellow Kid* color cartoon every Sunday that filled an entire page, and the cartoon also made several weekly appearances in black and white. Although Outcault's earliest *Yellow Kid* strips were only one panel, on October 25, 1896, he used multiple panels for the first time in *The Yellow Kid and His New Phonograph*. In later cartoons

COLOR PRINTING SPARKED THE COMICS

In the late nineteenth century, improved color printing was one reason for the birth of newspaper comic strips. Color printing was such a novelty then that people bought newspapers out of curiosity just to see color drawings. Most big cities in this era had multiple newspapers that battled each other to win readers. Comic strips, especially the Sunday color comics sections, became a weapon newspapers used to steal readers from their competitors. One reason Winsor McCay's *Little Nemo in Slumberland* is one of the most praised comic strips ever was his superb use of color. But comic strip historian Richard Marschall claims color also sparked the imaginations of other cartoonists:

> The cartoonists at the turn of the century lived in an astonishing environment. There was a feeling of intense artistic excitement as artists had a format of technical brilliance—the color of those early [comics] sections was superior to today's—the support of generous publishers, and a receptive public. [McCay's] stunning artwork was enhanced by superlative color printing technology [and] was the first comic strip to rely on sophisticated coloring techniques.

Richard Marschall. *America's Great Comic-Strip Artists: From the Yellow Kid to Peanuts.* New York: Stewart, Tabori and Chang, 1997, p. 13.

Outcault also unveiled a device unique to comics—the speech balloon—to show what the Kid was saying. However, at the same time, Outcault continued his previous practice of showing dialogue or enhancing the strip's narrative by writing on the Kid's nightshirt. In the first panel his shirt reads, "I listen to de woids of wisdom wot de phonograff will give you."[15]

Other Historic Comic Strips

In *Children of the Yellow Kid*, Harvey writes that the importance of Outcault's work was that it proved there was a huge audience for such art: "*The Yellow Kid* was the first comics character to demonstrate, beyond all question or quibble, the enormous appeal of the comics."[16] The strip's success led other newspapers to begin running comic strips. On December 12, 1897, *The Katzenjammer Kids* debuted in the *New York Evening Journal*. The *New York World* and the *New York Evening Journal* were competing for readers, and the *Journal* started its strip to lure readers who liked the new art form. *The Katzenjammer Kids* strip was created and drawn by Rudolph Dirks and featured two mischievous young German boys named Hans and Fritz who always got into trouble by playing pranks on adults. It was loosely based on Busch's *Max and Moritz*.

As more and more newspapers jumped on the comics bandwagon, some remarkable new strips appeared. On October 15, 1905, the *New York Herald* began running Winsor McCay's *Little Nemo in Slumberland*, one of the most artistic and imaginative comic strips of all time. McCay's lavish drawings brought to life a strange, sometimes frightening dream world full of weird architecture and whimsical characters unlike anything anyone had ever seen. McCay varied the size of the panels to create a distorted sense of reality or to change the perspective of the scene. He would even place thin panels the height of the entire page next to regular-sized panels. Comic art historian Roger Sabin writes: "[McCay] used a more sophisticated rendering style [than Outcault] to tell the story of a child from a well-to-do-family, and the wild dreams he has. [His] use of perspective and color were astounding, as was the way in which panels were structured in a cinematic fashion."[17]

Little Nemo in Slumberland by Winsor McCay, which began running in 1905, was known for its detailed, imaginative drawings and its innovative use of varied panel sizes.

The first daily comic strip was *A. Mutt*, which debuted on November 15, 1907, on the sports pages of the *San Francisco Chronicle*. The historical significance of this strip is that it was the first to be published daily and tell stories that continued from day to day. Drawn by Harry Conway "Bud" Fisher, the strip was better known later as *Mutt and Jeff* and featured the antics of two men, one tall and one short, who bet on horses.

The number of comic strips continued to grow, and by January 13, 1912, they had become so popular that the *New*

York Evening Journal began the first daily comics page. Before that, most comics pages had appeared only on Sunday or a few days during the week. The demand by readers for more and more comic strips spawned, almost by accident, a new type of comic art—comic books.

Comic Books

The Yellow Kid was so popular that in 1897 a 196-page hardcover collection of its comic strips was printed. There were several attempts at publishing comic strip material in magazine-style formats in the next few decades, including some that were tabloid-sized, measuring 10 by 15 inches (25.4cm by 38.1cm). None proved very successful until *Famous Funnies* No. 1 in July 1934, which sold for ten cents. Even though *Famous Funnies* and other early comic books were called comic magazines, they were the size of comic books today—$6^5/_8$ by $10^1/_4$ inches (16.8cm by 26cm). The sixty-eight-page comics consisted of reprints of popular comic strips like *Mutt and Jeff*, along with games, puzzles, and magic tricks.

People bought 180,000 copies of *Famous Funnies*, and its success launched a new outlet for comic art. In February 1935 *New Fun: The Big Comic Magazine* No. 1 was the first to feature original material. The cover—the only part printed in color—featured the first page of a Western story titled *Jack Woods*, drawn by Lyman Anderson. The thirty-six-page comic had a mixture of both humor and adventure stories. It sold well enough for a dime that its publisher, National Allied, continued publishing it. In the next few years, other companies began printing comic books.

Most comic books were simply new versions of various Western, adventure, and humor comic strips. Publishers hoped to increase their sales from comic books and were looking for a type of comic that could excite readers and provide a wider audience. They found it in a comic created by two young friends from Cleveland—writer Jerry Siegel and cartoonist Joe Shuster. Working together, they created the greatest of all comic book superheroes—Superman.

Siegel and Shuster made their debut in *New Fun* in 1936 with an adventure story about a French swordsman. In 1938 the company publishing *New Fun* wanted to create a new comic called *Action Comics*. Editor Vincent Sullivan wanted a blockbuster story to launch the new publication, and he found it in a comic strip that Siegel and Shuster had created but failed to sell to newspapers. Sullivan said, "It looked good. It

THE CREATORS OF SUPERMAN

Jerry Siegel and Joe Shuster began creating comic strips together while attending Glenville High School in Cleveland. Siegel wrote stories, and Shuster provided the drawings. In the summer of 1934 after they had graduated, Siegel spent a sleepless night imagining a new character that would become Superman. Siegel once said his desire to be big and strong so girls would notice him was the inspiration for the first comic book superhero: "As a high school student [I] had crushes on several attractive girls who either didn't know I existed or didn't care. It occurred to me—what if I was real terrific? What if I had something special going for me, like jumping over buildings or throwing cars around or something like that? Then maybe they would notice me."

That night Siegel wrote several weeks' worth of Superman stories for a proposed comic strip. He took them to Shuster, who brought Superman to life with his drawings. It would be four more years before their joint creation would hit newsstands in the first issue of *Action Comics*.

Quoted in Robert C. Harvey. *The Art of the Comic Book: An Aesthetic History*. Jackson: University Press of Mississippi, 1996, p. 19.

was different and there was a lot of action. This is what the kids wanted."[18] Sullivan asked Siegel and Shuster to rearrange the comic strip panels into a comic book story. Shuster said he and Siegel worked feverishly to do it, even though they had envisioned Superman as a comic strip: "We felt we had a great character and were determined [it] would be published."[19]

The cover of *Action Comics* No. 1 in June 1938 featured a strange-looking man in a tight-fitting blue costume and red cape who, impossibly, was holding an automobile high above his head. The vivid cover helped the first comic book superhero become an overnight sensation. Comic art historian Dennis Gifford claims that this unique new hero ensured the future of comic books: "[After Superman, comic books] have never been the same. For, more than creating a myth that threatens to resound through the eons via radio, television, and the movies, Superman created the comic book. Until he streaked over the horizon, comic books were but a reflection of strips that had gone before in newspapers."[20]

The daring originality that Superman brought to comic books lured millions of fans to the newest form of sequential art and pushed to new heights the creativity and imagination of other comic book artists.

Words and Pictures

It had taken several centuries for comic art to develop into comic strips. But in just a few years after the first strips appeared, they had become important to tens of millions of people, who faithfully read them every day. And just three decades later, comic books came along to once again expand the boundaries of comic art. Comic art historian Stephen Becker claims *The Yellow Kid* became popular because Outcault fused words and drawings so skillfully that he made readers realize the power of comic art: "With *The Yellow Kid* the words began to reflect the humor of the drawing, and vice versa, to the point—and an important point it was—*where neither was satisfactory without the other.*"[21]

The longer comic book format made that point even more dramatically to the millions of people who bought and read them. And during the rest of the twentieth century, these two new types of comic art exploded into the public consciousness in ways no one had dreamed possible.

Single-Panel Cartoons

Syd Hoff was one of the twentieth century's most prolific cartoonists. He was successful in two distinct categories of single-panel cartoons—comic as well as editorial/political. Hoff sold his first cartoon to the *New Yorker* magazine in 1930, when he was eighteen. His quirky sense of humor and deft drawing made him a star with the elite magazine famous for sophisticated cartoons. One of his early *New Yorker* pieces was set in a men's clothing store. There is no clothing in sight, and several salesmen stand idly in their underwear while one says to the others, "Most successful suit sale we ever had, I should say."[22]

In addition to drawing humorous cartoons and illustrating classic children's books like *Danny and the Dinosaur*, Hoff created powerful cartoons on social and political issues under the pen name A. Redfield. In one 1935 cartoon, a military veteran with medals pinned to his chest who had lost his legs while fighting in World War I is holding out a tin cup to an obviously rich man and woman standing before him. The woman, wearing pearls, says to her top-hatted husband, "Give him a nickel, sweetheart. After all, you made a couple of million [dollars] on the war."[23] The cartoon was a bitter comment about the disparity between a wealthy businessman who had profited from the war and an impoverished man who had fought in the conflict and paid a heavy price.

Hoff's message about the disparity between the lives of wealthy and average or poor people was so powerful and timeless that it was resurrected nearly eight decades later in November 2011, when Occupy movement protesters in Washington, D.C., used it in their newsletter. The Occupy movement staged protests across the nation to criticize the power and wealth the 1 percent of richest Americans have in comparison with average citizens.

Hoff explained once why he enjoyed using his drawing artistry to make such serious statements: "As for me, there are days when success as a comic artist is not enough. The urge to do battle with evil becomes irresistible. [With] a large letter 'S' (for Supercartoonist) emblazoned on my chest and a camelhair brush in my hand, I leap tall buildings and lay out crooks, corrupters,

Syd Hoff's 1938 cartoon set in a men's clothing store is one of the prolific artist's cartoons that appeared in the New Yorker.

"Most successful suit sale we ever had, I should say."

and warmongers."[24] The same spirit that led Hoff to expose what he believed was inequality between wealthy and poor Americans is what has motivated editorial cartoonists.

Cartoons to Make People Think

Cartoons that state a personal point of view on political or social issues are called editorial cartoons because they are similar to written editorials; they are also called political cartoons because so many of them comment directly on issues involving political figures or political parties. The idea of using art to express personal opinions, however, is much older than editorial cartoons. Artists for thousands of years have used sculptures, paintings, and other art forms to comment on every subject imaginable. In *Comic Art in America*, Stephen Becker claims that any work of art, to at least some degree, expresses a personal viewpoint:

> Any conventional, representational drawing says something about reality and implies a "point of view," even if the view expressed is simply that the object drawn is interesting. More often, the point is biased; there is a moral to the picture. The Renaissance Pieta was intended to express the artist's depth of feeling for—or even identification with—Jesus; it must also have been meant to arouse religious sentiment in the breast of the observer.[25]

The *Pietà*, which many consider to be the greatest work of Italian sculptor-painter Michelangelo, is a sculpture of Mary holding the body of Jesus after his death by crucifixion. The fifteenth-century statue has been reinterpreted by many sculptors and painters since then. But in all of them, the underlying message of Michelangelo's original work is clearly evident—a mother's grief over the death of her son combined with the significance of that death to Christians. As with the *Pietà*, graphic arts (like cartoons) can be a direct, immediate, and often more powerful way to express a point of view than by writing words, which take people longer to read and understand. Comic art historian Maurice Horn even claims that until the twentieth

BILL MAULDIN

Some of the twentieth century's finest editorial cartoons were drawn in the midst of war. Cartoonist Bill Mauldin won the Pulitzer Prize in 1945 for editorial cartoons he drew in Europe for the U.S. Army newspaper *Stars and Stripes*. Mauldin was a soldier as well as a cartoonist—a sergeant in the army's Forty-Fifth Division, he received a Purple Heart after being hit with a grenade fragment. Mauldin used humor to portray the reality of war in stunning, dramatic cartoons that humanized the combat experience of U.S. soldiers. The cartoon that won the Pulitzer had a caption that read: "Fresh, spirited troops, flushed with victory, are bringing in thousands of hungry, ragged, battle-weary prisoners. (News Item)." In the cartoon, a U.S. soldier walking alongside several prisoners in a driving rain looks as

weary and depressed as his prisoners. The cartoon contrasted sharply with many news stories that emphasized the glamour of war instead of its harsh reality. Mauldin's two main characters—Willie and Joe—were unshaven, unheroic-looking men who used humor to survive the physical danger and psychological turmoil of combat.

Quoted in Pulitzer Prizes. "Editorial Cartooning." www.pulitzer.org/bycat/Editorial-Cartooning.

Bill Mauldin, shown here, won a Pulitzer Prize in 1945 for his wartime editorial cartoons.

century, low levels of literacy in the United States and many other parts of the world made cartoons a more important way to influence people than written editorials:

> The time-honored cliché "A picture is worth a thousand words" never rang so true as during the latter part of the Nineteenth Century and most of the Twentieth, when competing doctrines and ideologies battled fiercely for the minds of people who were still largely illiterate. The potency of cartoon lay in its ability to make points sharply and quickly, without the semantic ambiguities inherent in the written word.[26]

English playwright Edward Bulwer-Lytton wrote in 1839, "The pen is mightier than the sword."[27] For many centuries and even today, pens wielded by cartoonists have often powerfully influenced public opinion. In the United States, cartoons were shaping American history even before the nation was created.

Historic Cartoon Commentary

Two cartoons were instrumental in influencing British colonists to fight during the Revolutionary War. Benjamin Franklin's *Join, or Die* cartoon of a snake cut into several parts, which is considered the first American editorial cartoon, helped convince British colonists they needed to band together to fight for their freedom. Becker writes, "[When] Franklin decided that the colonies would fail [in the war] without unity, he refrained from long essays and drew a cartoon, and his world knew exactly and immediately what he meant."[28]

Paul Revere is most famous for alerting colonial soldiers that the British army was advancing on them on April 19, 1775, prior to the Revolutionary War's first battles at Lexington and Concord, Massachusetts. But Revere, a skilled silversmith and engraver, also produced prints. On March 5, 1770, British soldiers killed five colonists who were protesting unfair British laws in what came to be known as the Boston Massacre. Revere's dramatic depiction of the event inflamed anti-British sentiment and helped push colonists closer to rev-

Thomas Nast's 1864 *Harper's Weekly* cartoon depicts the seemingly "useless" sacrifices of Union soldiers in the wake of a proposal by the Democratic Party to negotiate an end to the Civil War. This cartoon has been credited with rallying support behind the reelection of President Abraham Lincoln, a Republican.

olution. Revere's drawing was crude—the figures in it appear stiff and remarkably lifeless considering the event's dramatic nature. But comic art historian Harry Katz claims Revere's depiction of red-coated soldiers as "cold-hearted killers" is an example of how influential cartoons can be: "Widely distributed throughout the colonies, Revere's Bloody Massacre print dramatically displayed the power, immediacy, and effectiveness of political art."[29]

In 1864 President Abraham Lincoln partially owed his reelection victory to cartoonist Thomas Nast. Nast's cartoon *Compromise with the South*, which appeared in the September 3, 1864, edition of *Harper's Weekly*, shows a smiling Confederate soldier shaking hands with a bent-over, defeated-looking Union veteran with a wooden leg. The soldiers are standing over a grave whose tombstone reads, "In Memory of Union Heroes Who Fell in a Useless War."[30] The cartoon was critical of the Democratic Party's proposal to negotiate an end to the Civil War instead of fighting to win it militarily. The cartoon appeared two months before the election in which Lincoln faced Democratic candidate George McClellan, a Civil War general. It angered so many voters that many historians credit the cartoon with helping Lincoln win. Lincoln would later compliment Nast by calling him the Union's "best recruiting sergeant."[31]

*M*iguel Covarrubias was born in Mexico City, Mexico, in 1904. The talented artist nicknamed El Chamaco (the boy) moved to New York in 1924 at the age of nineteen. He and Al Hirschfeld invented the cartoon genre of celebrity caricature with stylish portraits of famous people. Their caricatures accented physical features of celebrities or placed them in unusual surroundings to comment on their personalities. Many Covarrubias caricatures were published in lush color in *Vanity Fair* magazine. One was of Emily Post, famous then for writing about etiquette. Caricature art historian Wendy Wick Reaves explains how his caricature mocked etiquette by showing Post drinking tea in an undignified pose:

> Covarrubias combined his ingredients [of caricature] with masterful draftsmanship and wit. [The] propped-up feet, spoon in the teacup, *Police Gazette*, and other details hilariously undermine the etiquette maven's reputation. But Covarrubias nails the portrayal through his draftsmanship: concentric shadows under the eyes, frizzy spirals in the hair, corny pastel hues, and the absurd crook of a little finger. Color, form, and composition always add to his humor and the ingenuity of his [work].

Quoted in Harry Katz, ed. *Cartoon America: Comic Art in the Library of Congress.* New York: Abrams, 2006, p. 180.

Nast was also a master of caricature, the art of altering the appearance of his subjects to make them look silly or comment on something they had done. He used this artistic weapon in cartoons in *Harper's Weekly* to spotlight the corruption of Democratic officials in New York City who had stolen millions of dollars in public funds. In a particularly powerful cartoon on September 23, 1871, titled *A Group of Vultures Waiting for the Storm to "Blow Over,"* Nast drew vultures with the heads of New York officials standing over bones that read, "New York City Treasury" and "tax payer."[32] Nast's cartoons are considered a major reason why William "Boss" Tweed, a former U.S. representative who headed the local Democratic Party, and other officials were convicted on corruption charges.

Other Historic Cartoons

Caricature was also a favorite way for cartoonists to portray presidents, whether they liked them or opposed them. For example, the image of President Abraham Lincoln appeared in countless cartoons. One of the most memorable Lincoln caricatures was by Frank Bellew in the November 26, 1864, edition of *Harper's Weekly*. Titled *Long Abraham Lincoln a Little Longer*, the excessively tall, narrow cartoon exaggerates Lincoln's six-foot-four-inch height and thinness. The visual impact of the drawing was Bellew's way of stating that Lincoln's reelection had made him into a bigger, more powerful political figure than he had been before.

Herbert Block, perhaps the twentieth century's most influential editorial cartoonist, was a talented and original artist whose humor and imaginative drawings made his work memorable. In cartoons signed "Herblock," he lampooned every president from Herbert Hoover to Bill Clinton. An April 3, 1956, *Washington Post* cartoon shows President Dwight Eisenhower wearing a fireman's hat, coat, and boots and telling a concerned-looking Uncle Sam, "Tsk Tsk—Somebody Should Do Something About That." They are looking through a window at several burning buildings with the phrase "Civil Rights Crisis"[33] embedded in towering flames. The cartoon was a caustic criticism of Eisenhower's unwillingness to use the power of the federal government to fight racial discrimination against African Americans.

African American cartoonist Oliver W. Harrington also attacked racism through cartoons. During the height of civil rights protests in 1965, a Harrington cartoon featured a black man with a bandaged head telling another, "Well, naturally I believe in nonviolence but the cops don't seem to know that!"[34]

Herbert Block, in his offices at the *Washington Post* in 1993, was perhaps the twentieth century's most influential editorial cartoonist.

It was a humorous yet poignant commentary on racist violence by white policemen against blacks who were peacefully protesting for their rights. When Harrington died in 1995, author and journalist Mel Watkins praised the powerful messages of Harrington's gritty, realistic cartoons, as well as their artistry: "Mr. Harrington is a gifted painter and fine artist. His drawings, unlike those of many cartoonists, often transcend mere caricature even as they convey the impressionistic vigor and ironic thrust demanded by the genre. As his cartoons demonstrate, much of his life and work was shaped by outrage at the way he and other blacks were treated."[35]

Throughout the long history of the United States, cartoonists have commented on every major issue and development in American life. Like Harrington, they often used humor to make their messages more acceptable and appealing. Despite this effort, the cartoonists risked making enemies of people who disagreed with them. Hoff once wrote, "Everybody can love a comic artist. Not everybody can love a political cartoonist. If you want to be loved by everybody, don't become a political cartoonist."[36] And artists who drew cartoons just to make people laugh have been loved by generations of readers because their cartoons made them smile.

Comic Cartoons

Until the last few decades of the nineteenth century, there were far more editorial and political cartoons than comic ones. Purely comic cartoons began gaining in popularity when technological developments allowed magazines to be printed in color. *Puck* in 1871 became the nation's first successful humor magazine, and it was soon joined by *Judge* and *Life*. Those magazines focused at first on political commentary but gradually began to run cartoons to make people laugh. The birth of comic strips in the 1890s made comic cartoons even more popular, and even more humorous cartoons began appearing in newspapers and magazines.

When the *New Yorker* began publication in 1925, one reason for its success was its many sophisticated cartoons. It has published nearly one thousand cartoons a year since then. John Held Jr. was an early *New Yorker* cartoonist. Held's drawings of fashionable young people of the 1920s are considered a definitive portrait of the decade. For most of the twentieth century, Al Hirschfeld, another *New Yorker* cartoonist, drew some of the best caricatures of Broadway stars and other celebrities. But Hirschfeld admits he was in awe of the "thin-line drawings" Held brought to cartooning: "This was something new and John was the first to use this style of drawing. His use of line communicated, determined the characters, created movement, and in turn defined the Roaring Twenties."[37]

The cover of an 1880 issue of *Puck* magazine features an editorial cartoon comparing candidates from the 1876 and 1880 presidential elections. *Puck* was the first successful humor magazine in the United States.

Famous *New Yorker* cartoonists include two who pushed the boundaries of cartoon humor with their infatuation with the macabre and strange—Charles Addams and Gahan Wilson. On January 7, 2012, Google honored Addams on the centennial of his birth by using the ghoulish characters from his *Addams Family* cartoons for a Google Doodle, the illustration that greets Internet users when they go to the Google page. Addams's cartoons were about members of a family who looked like characters from a scary movie. They featured the vampirish Morticia, the eccentric Gomez, two dark and brooding children named Wednesday and Pugsley, and various other relatives who made occasional appearances. The Addams family lived in a run-down, gothic-looking home and enjoyed all things gloomy, spooky, and morbid. The cartoons satirized family life and were so popular that they eventually spawned a television series, several movies, and a musical. In one cartoon, a man has just arrived at the Addams family's spooky-looking home with two pet carriers. Morticia yells to her husband, Gomez, "It's the children, darling, back from camp."[38] Addams began selling cartoons to the *New Yorker* in 1935, and he contributed to that and other magazines for five more decades.

Wilson also drew cartoons that emphasized the strange and bizarre for the *New Yorker* and other magazines. The nightmarish quality of Wilson's cartoons made the Addams family seem relatively normal. His use of bright colors, distorted wavy lines, and grimacing facial expressions created an atmosphere of menace and unreality. He often used monsters and scary situations to make twisted jokes. An example is one cartoon that has a small restaurant with a giant "EAT" sign on top of it as well as a giant green monster crawling toward it. Two people in the restaurant see the monster, and one of them wonders whether it can read, meaning that if it can, it will eat the restaurant.

Working in this same genre was one of the twentieth century's funniest and weirdest comic artists, Don Martin. He worked for a magazine called *Mad*, which was founded in 1952 and quickly became the nation's premier comic art magazine. From 1956 to 1988, Martin's quirky, hilarious, sometimes grotesque cartoons earned him the title of *Mad*'s Maddest Artist.

Most of Martin's characters shared a set of physical trademarks—pointy heads, huge jaws, giant noses, wiry hair, and feet that seemed to fold in half—that made his work instantly recognizable. Although Martin's characters often had laugh-out-loud names like Fester Bestertester, Martin delighted in torturing them with falling bricks, car crashes, and other physical mayhem that elastically contorted their features and bodies into strange, unique shapes. In *The Completely Mad Don*

Martin by Don Martin, Charles Taylor describes how Martin did this:

> Martin puts the bodies of these characters through every kind of permutation, treating them as much like gadgets as the squirting flowers and joy buzzers that populate his gags: glass eyes pop out from a pat on the back; heads are steamrollered into manhole-cover shapes. All of this accompanied by a Dadaist panoply of sound effects found nowhere else: shtoink! shklorp! fwoba-dap![39]

Martin's skillful drawings and quirky view of reality helped him create a unique alternate comic universe that people enjoyed returning to time and again—fans have purchased more than 7 million books featuring his cartoons. Martin was beloved because his work was so original. Wilson says that one of the attributes of great cartoonists like Martin is that they have a unique viewpoint they share with readers: "[That's] what makes them interesting. They make you think, 'Oh my God, I didn't realize that.' And there's nobody like 'em. I mean, Picasso wouldn't be Picasso without Cezanne, but Picasso was Picasso. It's very magical stuff."[40]

Cartoons Shape Culture

Although not everyone will like the work of a particular comic artist, some cartoon creations have been loved by so many people that they have become an integral part of American culture. In fact, inventive and imaginative cartoonists have created many characters that have become iconic symbols familiar to every American. Some of the most familiar came from the pens of editorial cartoonists such as Thomas Nast, who was born in Landau, Germany, on September 27, 1840, but moved to the United States with his family six years later. Despite being an immigrant, Nast is credited with creating the animal symbols for the nation's two political parties—the Democratic Party donkey and Republican Party elephant. Nast first caricatured the Democratic Party as a donkey in a cartoon in *Harper's Weekly* in 1870. Four years later Nast drew

Roz Chast

osalind "Roz" Chast is one of the few women to become a *New Yorker* staff cartoonist. The Brooklyn native sold her first cartoon in 1978. Her work, in both black-and-white and multiple colors, has appeared in many magazines since then. Chast has also illustrated books but says, "I just really love the cartoon form. I love the plasticity of it." In a 2011 interview, Chast explained where she gets ideas for her cartoons: "Sometimes it can be something personal that happened to me that can spark an idea for a cartoon. Sometimes it will be something somebody said. Sometimes it's just really—like a genre cartoon. Like gravestone cartoons. Like the end-of-the-world guys. They don't wear the white robes anymore except in cartoons, but I do see them. I see them in the subway, preaching hellfire."[1]

Chast penned a unique, ironic take on the many cartoons featuring end-of-the-world predictions. This cartoon has one robed man carrying a sign that reads, "The End Is Near," while a man standing next to him holds a sign that says, "You Wish."[2]

1. Quoted in Jessica Grose. "Questions for Roz Chast." *Slate*, October 17, 2011. www.slate.com/articles/arts/interrogation/2011/10/roz_chast_s_what_i_hate_the_new_yorker_cartoonist_discusses_her_.html.
2. Roz Chast. "Cartoons." http://rozchast.com/cartoons_fear.shtml.

Roz Chast's editorial cartoons have appeared in many magazines, including the New Yorker.

a rampaging elephant with "The Republican Vote"[41] on its side to symbolize the Republican Party.

It was another immigrant who first drew Uncle Sam, the figure that has been used to represent the United States in editorial cartoons for more than 150 years. Frank Bellew was born to an English family in India on April 18, 1828, and came to the United States in 1850. He became a prolific cartoonist and founded several humor magazines, including *Lantern* and *Vanity Fair*. Uncle Sam had been a nickname for the United States since 1820, but Bellew was the first to portray him in human form, in a cartoon in the March 13, 1852, issue of *Lantern*. Other cartoonists began to draw Uncle Sam, too, including Nast. In *Uncle Sam's Thanksgiving Dinner* in *Harper's Weekly* on November 28, 1869, Nast drew Uncle Sam carving a turkey to feed people gathered around a large table, including African Americans, Chinese, and other immigrants. The cartoon was one of many in which Nast supported the rights of minorities.

However, it was James Montgomery Flagg, who was born in Pelham Manor, New York, who created the definitive patriotic figure of Uncle Sam. That historic caricature emerged during World War I in a drawing on the July 6, 1916, cover of *Leslie's Weekly*. Flagg, who began selling cartoons to magazines when he was only fourteen, gave Uncle Sam his now familiar wispy white beard, red tie, formal coat with tails, and top hat with stars. In the drawing, Uncle Sam points his finger and glares directly at the reader while a line beneath him asks, "What Are You Doing for Preparedness?"[42] The drawing was supposed to make Americans think about what to do to prepare for fighting in the war. The iconic image was so powerful that the U.S. government changed the words to "I Want You for the U.S. Army"[43] and made more than 4 million copies of it as a poster to recruit soldiers.

One of the biggest presents cartoonists ever gave U.S. children was the image of Santa Claus. Nast borrowed from both Clement Moore's 1823 poem "The Night Before Christmas" and the Saint Nicholas tradition from his native Germany to create the first cartoon image of Santa Claus. The historic

cartoon appeared on the cover of the January 3, 1863, edition of *Harper's Weekly*. Titled *Santa Claus in Camp*, it shows Santa handing out presents to children and soldiers in a Union army camp. Historian R.J. Brown writes that Nast added to Santa lore in the many Santa drawings he later produced: "He was the first to establish that Santa's home was in the North Pole [and the] concept of Santa having a workshop and elves to help him were also Nast's idea. The custom of sending Santa a letter is also due to Thomas Nast."[44]

Comic cartoonists have also shaped culture with their funny, sometimes acid comments about life and culture. Leading the way was *Mad*, which in 1972 had 2 million subscribers. *New Yorker* cartoonist and graphic novelist Art Spiegelman once claimed that with its brash, bold satires of politics and other phases of culture, "Mad was more important than [any other factor] in shaping the generation that protested the Vietnam War." He also said, "It opened cartoonists up to what the possibilities of the medium were. It showed how zany comics could be."[45]

"Graphic Snapshots of Our Times"

The Library of Congress is the largest library in the world and includes a vast collection of original comic art. James H. Billington was appointed the thirteenth Librarian of Congress in September 1987 and in 2012 still held that position. In the foreword to *Cartoon America: Comic Art in the Library of Congress*, Billington writes that cartoons have played an important part in the nation's history and cultural life:

> Cartoon art, a truly democratic art for a democratic society, has always played a special role in America. Cartoons have helped spark revolution, sway election campaigns, reveal corruption, and promote reform. They educate and entertain, inform and enlighten. Artful or awful, they are the graphic snapshots of our times, spontaneous and accessible to all. [Like] jazz and baseball, they are an indigenous part of American culture.[46]

3

Comic Strips

Comic strips spread across the nation quickly after *The Yellow Kid* debuted in the *New York World* on February 17, 1895. When other newspapers asked *World* publisher William Randolph Hearst for permission to reprint the strip, Hearst sold it to them in a practice known as syndication. Other newspapers began hiring their own cartoonists to draw strips, and in the next century more than two hundred different comic strips and daily cartoon panels were created. Not everyone, however, loved comic strips. Some people believed the comical stories that made people laugh—the very reason people read them!—were juvenile and taking up space that could be used for more important material. Typical of this backlash was an editorial in the *Boston Herald* in 1908: "The comic section has had its day. The funnies are not funny anymore and they have become vulgar in design and tawdry in color. [Most] discerning persons throw them aside without inspection, experience having taught them that there is no hope for improvement in these gaudy sheets."[47]

The editorial grossly misjudged two key factors regarding comic strips—their popularity and the creativity and inventiveness comic artists would bring to them in the future to make them even better. This was especially true of *Krazy Kat*, a strip that appeared five years later, on October 13, 1913, and would run for more than three decades.

A Comic Strip Genius

The February 1999 edition of the *Comics Journal*, a magazine devoted to comic art, compiled a list of the one hundred best comic strips, comic books, and graphic novels. Topping the list was *Krazy Kat* by George Herriman. In addition to being the first African American comic strip artist, Herriman was one of the most creative pioneers of the new art form; many historians even consider him the greatest comic strip artist ever. When it debuted in 1905, Winsor McCay's *Little Nemo* was praised for his creative use of space, such as having panel lines explode apart when a character sneezed. But in *Masters of American Comics*, John Carlin writes that Herriman's work was more artistic: "Herriman's inventive use of panels and page layouts is the gold standard in comics to this day. [He] took McCay's use of multiple layers of graphic information and expanded it into layers of ideas through a unique blend of language, design, ideas, and drawing. This gave *Krazy Kat* a profound quality that is difficult to find in the best art or literature, much less in comics."[48]

An example of Herriman's graphic genius is his Sunday strip for November 3, 1918. Herriman divided an entire page into eight diagonal slices running downward at a 45-degree angle from right to left to simulate a hill. In the first panel Ignatz Mouse urges Krazy Kat to push a boulder down the hill. In the second panel, Ignatz tells Krazy Kat to follow the speeding boulder, which in succeeding panels knocks down trees and smashes through buildings before coming to a halt. After Krazy trudges back up the hill, Ignatz asks him if the boulder had gathered any moss. Krazy says no, which satisfies Ignatz, who is trying to prove the truth of the ancient adage "A rolling stone gathers no moss."

Despite the fact that the strip's main characters were a cat, mouse, and a dog in a police officer's uniform named Offisa Bull Pup, *Krazy Kat* was not a vehicle for juvenile jokes. The

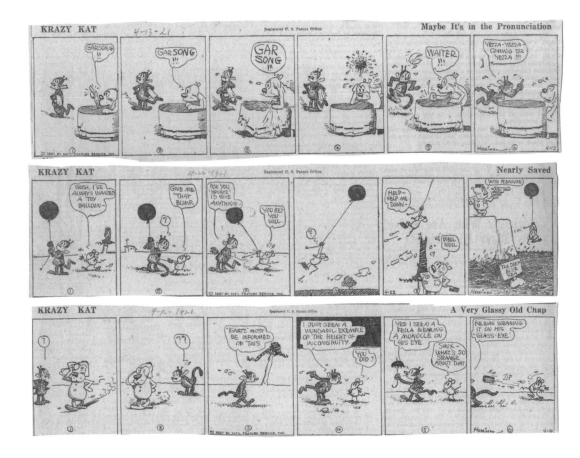

simple, absurd ending to the dramatic full-page strip cited above was typical of Herriman's sly, intellectual punch lines. His strip was often compared to jazz—a creative and complex new style of music then becoming popular—because of his inventive graphics and amusing dialogue. This is how one journalist described it:

> The Kat speaks a dialect that is distinctive, yet elastic, and impossible to pinpoint. Yiddish? "Ooy-y-y—Sotch a noive." Creole? "S'funna, but I dun't see no stomm— the sky is klee—blue an' bride wit' sunshine—not a cloud in it." Brooklyn-Italian? "Jess fency, Offissa Pupp, the tree of us, riding around tigedda—like boom kimpenions." At one point, Krazy asks Ignatz: "Why is lenguage?" and then answers the question: "Lenguage is that we may mis-unda-stend each udda."[49]

Three 1921 *Krazy Kat* comic strips depict the adventures of Krazy, Ignatz, and Pup, who were the creation of George Herriman, the first African American comic strip artist.

George Herriman was the first African American comic strip artist. However, no one knew this until 1971, when research showed that he had been born to mixed-race parents on August 22, 1880, in New Orleans. His family moved to California to escape racism when Herriman was a child. He was so light skinned that he was able to live as a white person. Ironically, Herriman's first comic strip, *Music Mose*, was about a black man who often pretended to be white. In his debut on February 17, 1902, Mose pretended to be Scottish, only to be beaten and have his bagpipe wrecked. English journalist Sarah Boxer writes about how Herriman toyed with race in that strip:

> Oddly, he made cartoons that seem a little racist themselves. In 1902, Herriman drew a [comic strip] called *Musical Mose*, in which a black man repeatedly tries and fails to "impussanate" a white man. In one installment, Mose masquerades as a Scotsman. Some white women discover he's black and beat him up. Mose moans, "I wish mah color would fade." His wife is unsympathetic: "Why didn't yo impussanate a cannibal?" she asks.

Sarah Boxer. "Herriman: Cartoonist Who Equalled Cervantes." *Telegraph* (London), July 7, 2007. www .telegraph.co.uk/culture/books/3666365/Herriman-Cartoonist-who-equalled-Cervantes.html.

Herriman's comic strip featured desert scenery from the American Southwest that often shifted from panel to panel in no apparent pattern, something that delighted readers because they never knew what to expect. It also featured perhaps the strangest love-hate triangle in any fictional work. Countless strips featured Ignatz trying to hit Krazy in the head with a brick while Pup tried to protect the cat. The brick was Ignatz's strange way of showing he loved Krazy, who never minded being beaned because he liked the mouse. In another twist on animal behavior, Pup guarded Krazy because he also liked him.

These mind-bending relationships, the strip's visual attractiveness, and its innovative language combined to make *Krazy Kat* a fan favorite and an artistic triumph. In his 1924 book about new forms of art, famed cultural critic Gilbert Seldes proclaims that "KRAZY KAT, the daily comic strip of George Herriman is, to me, the most amusing and fantastic and satisfactory work of art produced in America today."[50] Comic art historians continue to praise Herriman today because he invented so many creative new ways to tell stories.

The ability to tell stories in interesting ways is why people love comic strips. But doing that is an art in itself.

Sequential Art in Comic Strips

Comic art genius Will Eisner invented the term *sequential art* and has written about it more knowledgably than anyone has. In *Graphic Storytelling and Visual Narrative*, Eisner stresses that the purpose of graphic design is not to wow the reader but to tell a coherent story. "Despite the high visibility and attention that artwork compels, I hold that the story is the most critical component in a comic," he says. "Not only is it the intellectual frame on which all artwork rests, but it, more than anything else, helps the work endure."[51]

Because most comic strips have multiple panels, artists have to learn how to dramatically and effectively tell their stories across a series of confined spaces. They also have to pace the flow of their stories over the number of panels available— three or four in a weekday strip but more in larger Sunday versions. This is true whether they are combining images and words into a graphic joke or narrating a continuing adventure. Robert C. Harvey explains how pacing the action adds another dimension of reality to comic strips: "If speech balloons give comic strips their life, then breaking the narrative into successive panels gives that life duration, an existence beyond a moment. The breakdown of the action is to comics what time is to life. In fact, 'timing'—pace as well as duration—is the direct result of sequencing pictures to make up a comic strip."[52]

One key way artists make their work interesting is to change the perspective of the reader's view in each panel, much as movies do; some panels show scenes from further away while others zoom in to capture facial expressions or key action. Stephen Becker claims Hal Foster did this better than almost anyone in his epic strip *Prince Valiant*: "From a long shot of soldiers struggling up a hillside he may turn to a close-up of his terrified [heroine's] lips parted in fear as she watches her knight go forth."[53] Comic strip artists also toyed with reader perspective through extreme close-ups that magnified the size of objects. Coulton Waugh writes that McCay did this masterfully in his *Little Nemo* strip: "In wild exaggeration of depth, of the contrast between a pea and a planet, of the enormity of a giant mouth—in which one pulls a tooth by dynamiting it out—McCay has had no equal, before or since."[54]

Comic artists make their work interesting in a number of ways, including varying the size of panels and toying with the lines that delineate them. In 1994 Patrick McDonnell began *Mutts*, a strip about the friendship of Earl (a dog) and Mooch (a cat). In the strip from December 7, 2011, when another cat asks Earl where Mooch is, Earl replies, "He's thinking outside the box."[55] In a graphic play on the popular phrase about thinking creatively, Mooch is seated outside the black-lined panel (box) containing Earl and the other cat. McDonnell also drew swirling lines above Mooch's head to show that he is thinking. This is one of the many symbols cartoonists use as graphic shorthand to show what characters are doing or what is happening to them. Other examples are small stars to indicate pain or a saw cutting through wood that simulates snoring to show someone is asleep. Comic historian Richard Marschall explains that this is an important part of the graphic creativity comic artists use to tell stories:

> The comics' vocabulary transcends the written words of balloons and captions: it extends—expands—to unique and meaningful signs and symbols: motion lines, sweat beads, stars of pain, sound-effect indications, all hovering physically within the comic-strip universe. They are not crutches for the cartoonist but splendid means to tell stories in a different way from, say, the novelist.[56]

Bud Fisher used panels of varying sizes and sound effects like "SMACK" to tell a story and create visual interest in a 1923 *Mutt and Jeff* comic.

Artists incorporate sound into their strips with words like "BANG!" for a gunshot or "BOOM!" for an explosion. Both were used repeatedly in adventure strips of the 1930s and 1940s, which ushered in a golden age of comic strips.

Adventure Instead of Laughs

Many comic historians claim the adventure comic strip era began on January 7, 1929, when *Tarzan* and *Buck Rogers* debuted in newspaper comic sections, which were known as "the funnies" because most strips were dedicated to making people laugh. The new strips featured the dangerous exploits of an

English lord raised by apes and a futuristic spaceman. Other adventure strips soon followed, like *Flash Gordon*, *Dick Tracy*, and *Terry and the Pirates*.

Adventure strips are also considered continuity strips because they tell stories over several weeks, which was rare before then. Cartoonist Al Capp's historic *Li'l Abner*, which debuted on August 13, 1934, and ran until November 13, 1977, was a hybrid of humor and adventure strips because he put his hillbilly hero in dangerous but comical situations. Capp once explained why adventure strips dominated newspaper comics for more than two decades: "Newspapers publishers had discovered that people bought more papers, more regularly, if they were *worried* by a comic strip than if they were merely amused by one. [That] poor soul couldn't wait until dawn came and with it the next edition, to relieve his agony."[57]

Artists used cliff-hangers, a literary device common in books and films, to make people keep reading their strips. They would put characters in danger or create other dramatic situations in the final panel of each day's episode to make people want to know what happened next. Several adventure comic artists also brought a new artistry to comic strips. In *The Smithsonian Collection of Newspaper Comics*, Bill Blackbeard and Martin Williams write that because of adventure strips, "the comic strip was seen at its most varied, inventive, colorful and exciting in the thirties and early forties—a peak of creativity and popularity it has not held since."[58]

Adventure Strip Masters

One of the finest adventure strip cartoonists was Hal Foster. Foster admired Howard Pyle, who illustrated books about fictional heroes like Robin Hood and whose work was a blend of realism and hero worship of the figures he drew. Foster was a fine artist whose work looked more like paintings than cartoons. He made *Tarzan* memorable with vibrant, dramatic drawings of characters, action-packed scenes, and lush, exotic backgrounds. Stephen Becker writes, "Here was an artist not in the comics tradition at all, but rather in the [tradition of] book illustrators. . . . [Some] single panels in *Prince Valiant*

Dick Tracy

On October 4, 1932, Chester Gould brought the grim realism of crime to the comic page with *Dick Tracy*. His square-jawed, heroic policeman has been fighting crime and fascinating readers ever since. The world Gould created was dark and forbidding, the violence real, and the criminals twisted and evil. The historic strip spawned many imitations. But comic art historian Richard Marschall claims no one was ever able to scare readers like Gould:

> Expressionism in the funnies is what the detective strip *Dick Tracy* was: grotesqueries in character traits, depictions, and actions; a rogue's gallery of bizarre villains; and stark black-and-white contrasts. If evil is ugly, believed cartoonist Chester Gould, it should look ugly. In Gould's world, cityscapes were severe, farmlands foreboding, and danger lurked around every darkened corner and shadowed alley. Black and white was his moral code as well as his preferred mode of expression; even Sunday pages were colored in flat tones, without nuances or shading. Famous Tracy villains included Flattop, the Mole, Stooge Viller, Mumbles, B-B Eyes [and] the Brow.

Richard Marschall. "The Newspaper Comic Strip—One of the Most Truly American Art Forms—Celebrates Its Centennial This Year." *American History*, September–October 1995, p. 34.

Chester Gould created the Dick Tracy *comic in 1932.*

must have taken longer to draw than entire Sunday strips of other comics."[59] Foster gained room to create dramatic scenes by running narrative and dialogue at the bottom or top of each panel instead of using speech balloons. This device also gave the strip a more literary feel.

Three years later Foster abandoned his *Tarzan* strip, which was based on a character from books by Edgar Rice Burroughs, so he could create a different type of hero. As Foster explains, "I wanted to [find] someplace to hang a story that was sort of fantasy and fairy tale."[60] The place for Foster's new hero was as a knight in King Arthur's court. *Prince Valiant* was an instant success when it hit the comic pages on February 13, 1937. Foster's artistry was so impressive that he was eventually elected to Great Britain's Royal Society of Arts, a rare honor for a cartoonist. The strip has remained popular, and other artists were still producing *Prince Valiant* for Sunday pages in 2012, three decades after Foster died.

Although Foster's work influenced many artists, historian Waugh claims, "The man was so good at his particular job that there remained little for subsequent workers to improve on."[61] One who came close was Alex Raymond, who on January 7, 1934, penned the first installment of *Flash Gordon*. *Buck Rogers* by Philip Francis Nowlan was the first space-oriented strip but was poorly drawn while *Flash Gordon* earned Raymond a reputation as one of the great comic strip masters.

The strip's main characters were the heroic spaceman Flash, sensuous Dale Arden, and stately Dr. Zarkov. Raymond brought them to life in vivid detail, and his action scenes jumped off the page. Don Moore, a fiction writer who collaborated with Raymond on the comic strip *Jungle Jim*, explains the power of Raymond's drawing: "His exquisite renderings—his fantastic locales, gorgeously sexy women, and ruggedly handsome men—gave the space opera so persuasive an illusion of reality that Flash Gordon became a part of the American cultural heritage."[62]

Another fine artist was Milt Caniff, whose *Terry and the Pirates* debuted on December 9, 1934. Set in the Far East, it

featured the exploits of a young American boy named Terry Lee and his rugged reporter friend Pat Ryan. The strip had exotic locales and strange characters like Big Stoop, a nine-foot-tall Mongolian who helps them, and the Dragon Lady, a gorgeous pirate who is their enemy. Comic strip historian John Carlin hails Caniff as the "Master of Suspense" and claims Caniff brought together elements of early adventure strips into one visually powerful classic form: "Caniff's use of framing, blocking, and juxtaposed angles of vision to create montagelike effects was unmatched. He was the first comic artist to completely control his reader's point of view and did so to convey a sense of realism and urgency that was tremendously influential on artists in the comic book era."[63]

Although adventure strips were among the most popular comic strips in the 1930s and 1940s, millions of people still loved humor strips. Amazingly, Alex Raymond also played a role in creating one of the most iconic female humor stars—Blondie.

A 1941 panel from the comic strip *Terry and the Pirates* presents one of the many exotic adventures of a young American boy and his reporter friend.

Comic art historian Robert C. Harvey believes Milt Caniff was one of the greatest and most influential comic strip artists. Caniff drew *Terry and the Pirates* from 1934 until 1946, when he left to create a new comic strip called *Steve Canyon*, which he continued to create until his death in 1988. Harvey claims Caniff made himself great by improving during the run of *Terry and the Pirates*:

> [Caniff] shifted from pen to brush and cloaked his drawings in shadow [to achieve] a stunning illusion of reality. [His] chiaroscuro [treatment of light and shadow] technique was widely imitated by those cartoonists doing adventure strips who were not aping [Alex] Raymond or [Hal] Foster. [He] evolved the chiaroscuro treatment into something considerably more complex than depicting the play of light and shadow. Shadows are still brushed in on the sides of figures and objects away from the light source but all wrinkles in clothing, for instance, are rendered with heavy brush strokes whether they are on the "shadow side" of a figure or not. [His] modification of the technique sustained the same visual effect of high contrast between black and white, but the artwork is now much blacker than earlier.

Robert C. Harvey. *Children of the Yellow Kid*. Seattle: Frye Art Museum, 1998, p. 90.

Milt Caniff draws Steve Canyon at a comedy festival in 1953.

Making People Laugh

The real artistry of humor strip artists was in making people laugh and love their characters. None of these characters was more beloved than Murat "Chic" Young's Blondie. When she debuted on September 8, 1930, she was a flapper—a term in that era for a fun-loving, beautiful young woman—named Blondie Boopadoop. Strips about young women were popular then because they were beginning to assert their independence in a male-dominated society. However, *Blondie* did not become one of the most popular comic strips until February 7, 1937, when Young had Blondie marry Dagwood Bumstead. The family-oriented strip became such a beloved classic that it was still being published eight decades later.

Young's daughter, Jeanne Young O'Neil, says of her father that "[his] genius was in seeing the moment of greatest humor in a [situation], knowing how and when to embellish or simplify [it], and how to cap it off with a rib-tickling punch line."[64] Although Young's humor and not his art made the strip memorable, Blondie is drawn in a style that makes her unforgettable. And Raymond was partly responsible for that. Like many cartoonists, Young employed other artists to help him draw daily and Sunday strips. While working as Young's assistant in the early 1930s, Raymond is credited with influencing Young to give Blondie a sexier figure and more realistic appearance than Dagwood and their children, Alexander and Cookie.

There were many types of humor strips. Popular characters from animated cartoons starred in comic strips, including Felix the Cat, Mickey Mouse, Betty Boop, Donald Duck, and Bugs Bunny. In the 1940s the term *teenager* became popular as a way to recognize that young people between childhood and adulthood had their own unique culture. Several comic strips had teenage characters as their stars, including *Archie*, which began in 1942 and is still being published.

Some of the most popular comic strips featured children, including *Nancy* (1933), *Henry* (1934), and *Little Lulu* (1950). Henry, a young bald-headed boy eternally clad in T-shirt and

A collector holds a copy of the first *Archie* comic book, published in 1942. The antics of Archie and his teenage pals have been presented as a comic strip for several decades.

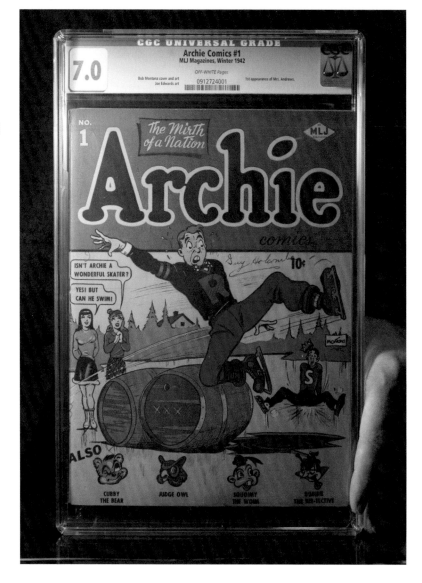

shorts, was one of a handful of mute comic art characters. Henry became popular in 1932 through *Saturday Evening Post* cartoons. Ironically, cartoonist Carl Anderson's decision to render Henry speechless even though other characters in his cartoons sometimes spoke helped him migrate to newspapers. *Henry* reprints were popular in foreign countries because there was little or no English dialogue to translate. When newspaper czar William Randolph Hearst saw *Henry* in a German publication, he signed Anderson for King Features, his company that syndicated comic strips. Wordless Henry was still being published more than eighty years later.

The most famous child star in the comics was *Little Orphan Annie*, a brave little girl with red curls who was always accompanied by her faithful dog Sandy. During adventures that began on August 5, 1924, and continued through June 13, 2010, when the strip ended, Annie never blinked an eye at the many dangers she faced. That was because she did not have any eyes. Cartoonist Harold Gray substituted blank ovals that showed no expression for her eyes and those of most other characters. It may have been because Gray was a mediocre artist—Al Capp once cruelly claimed that figures in *Little Orphan Annie* had "all the vitality of Easter Islands statues"[65]—but the strange white spaces had the curious power to draw the reader's attention to Annie more powerfully than artistically rendered eyes. What made the strip memorable was its unique blend of humor—Annie was prone to exclaiming, "Leapin' lizards!"[66]—and adventure. And that was something Capp's work shared with Gray's.

Humor, Danger, and Satire

Capp dreamed as a child of drawing a comic strip that made people laugh. But he said that the popularity of adventure strips made him add danger to *Li'l Abner*: "Therefore the situations [I create] are macabre, horrible, thrilling and chilling [while] the characters' naïve solutions and reactions to these problems provide the comedy that makes me happy."[67] Abner lived in Dogpatch, a poverty-stricken southern town populated by characters memorable either for their grotesque appearance or weird names, such as Joe Btfsplk, the world's unluckiest man who had a name no one could pronounce and a black cloud constantly hovering over his head. There was also Daisy Mae, a gorgeous young blonde woman that Abner wed in 1952 after evading her every effort to snare him for nearly two decades, and Mammy Yokum, Abner's scrawny but lethally strong mother.

In one of the silly but dangerous adventures Capp invented, nearly everyone in Dogpatch died of hunger when turnip termites had destroyed their turnips. It was their only cash crop, and the disaster made everyone too poor to buy food. The near tragedy was manufactured by wealthy Lumpington Van Dump to force Daisy to marry him. When Daisy consented to marry Van Dump to save her beloved Abner, he airlifted food to Dogpatch. In one of the strange twists of fate Capp created to rescue Abner from dire situations, Van Dump fell down an elevator shaft before he could marry Daisy.

Capp, the son of Russian immigrants, had grown up poor and resented rich people. The termite episode was one of many in which Capp satirized the excesses and selfishness of the rich. Capp poked fun at them by creating characters such as General Bullmoose, a greedy businessman. In *America's Great Comic-Strip Artists*, Marschall writes: "Al Capp was not a master satirist who happened to draw funny pictures. He was, proudly and fiercely, a cartoonist who happened to

do what he did better than virtually anyone else in the select circle of comic-strip masters—and with a real sense of himself and his times."[68]

Comic Strip Appeal

Brian Walker has helped continue two popular strips his dad, Mort Walker, created—*Beetle Bailey* and *Hi and Lois*—and written extensively on comic strip history. Walker believes the reason comic strips have survived as a beloved cultural institution is that readers connect with them emotionally. "The funnies have endured primarily because comic characters have a universal, timeless appeal," he says. "Their daily appearances make them familiar to millions, their triumphs make them heroic. Their struggles make them seem human. Cartoonists create friends for their readers."[69]

4

Comic Books

The comic book format popular around the world today began with publication of early prototypes such as *Famous Funnies* in July 1934 and *New Fun* in February 1935. This new type of comic art enabled artists to tell stories over multiple pages and was a great leap forward artistically from comic strips. However, the new format was challenging because artists had to learn to adjust the flow of their stories and manage images and words in a creative way that would hold the reader's interest over many pages.

Legendary comic artist Will Eisner helped pioneer comic book art. He is widely respected for the inventiveness and creativity he brought to *The Spirit*, a comic book about a mysterious, masked crime fighter he wrote and drew from 1940 until 1952. Eisner writes that the early years of comic books were exciting because artists were literally inventing a new form of comic art: "We had to master the language of the genre: comics have their own grammar, alphabet and discipline. To get the most out of the technique we had to learn what worked in a frame and what didn't. Which symbols conveyed meaning most efficiently? How could the physical requirements of the cartoon, the frames and dialogue balloons, be used as forceful visual elements?"[70]

Eisner and other artists experimented with everything, especially the size and number of panels per page; some panels extended the width of a page or dropped down vertically to the bottom to frame other, smaller panels. Artists simulated blood dripping from dialogue lettering to express horror their characters felt or drew jagged edges around dialogue balloons to show shock or fear.

It took time to learn such artistic tricks, and early comic books looked a lot like comic strips. The superhero genre of comics books, devoted to characters like Superman and Batman, was the one that shaped comic book style the most in its infancy and helped make the new style of comic art popular.

A Superhero Invasion

When Superman debuted in *Action Comics* in June 1938, the last panel of his first story ended with, "And so began the startling adventures of the most sensational character of all time."[71] That may sound overly dramatic, but comic art historian Robert C. Harvey claims Superman's debut was historically important because "it transformed the infant comic book industry."[72] Comic book publishers were struggling to attract readers to make the new art form profitable, but Superman was so popular that fans were soon buying five hundred thousand copies of each issue of *Action Comics*. In 1939 when Superman got a comic book all to himself, sales of *Superman* soared even higher and by 1950 averaged 1.25 million copies a month.

Superman became popular because he was a superhero, a new type of character that fired the imaginations of millions of readers. His first adventures, however, were not an artistic success. Joe Shuster, the artist who first drew Superman, had no formal art training, and many comic art historians consider his drawings primitive. The first images of Superman that he created in 1938 had indistinct facial features and a lack of detail in his musculature; even the iconic *S* emblem on his chest was barely recognizable. Cartoonist and comic art historian Jules Feiffer writes, "His work was direct, unprettied—crude and vigorous. [He] could not draw well, but he drew simplemindedly."[73]

However, comic art historian Ron Goulart claims that Shuster's artistic failings were overshadowed by his creativity in manipulating the comic book format: "Shuster was among the first to realize that a comic book page is not a newspaper page. He broke his [pages] up in new and interesting ways and was one of the first comic book artists to use a full-page splash panel to lead off his stories."[74] Feiffer concurs with this assessment. He also praises Shuster for the exciting way he composed action scenes: "Superman running up the sides of dams, leaping over anything that stood in his way [or] cleaning and jerking two-ton get-away cars [of criminals] and pounding them into the side of cliffs."[75] Shuster was also a master of mixing long and close-up views in his panels, a technique he borrowed from movies.

Shuster's Superman does not look like the traditional image most people remember from comic books. The reason is that Shuster was so busy overseeing stories in several comic books featuring Superman plus a newspaper comic strip that began on January 16, 1939, that he needed assistants to help him draw the various publications. Wayne Boring was the best of Shuster's assistants. He was so good that by 1942 he was the main artist for *Superman* and *Action Comics*. Thus it is Boring's drawn interpretation of the Man of Steel that became classic. Comic art historian Les Daniels describes Boring's Superman: "Massive [far more muscular than Shuster's] and magisterial with a suggestion of middle age, Boring's Superman was a paternalistic hero distinctly different from the exuberant character of a few years earlier. Wayne Boring drew the Man of Steel for over a quarter of a century and in the process he defined the world's first superhero for a generation."[76] Superman was the first superhero, but it was not long before he was joined by dozens of others.

New Superheroes

The May 1939 cover of *Detective Comics* featured a mysterious figure swinging on a rope high over the rooftops of a big city, his cape with bat-like wings spread out behind him. It was Batman, who like Superman is still a popular superhero.

Unlike Superman, Batman has no superpowers. Instead, Batman battles criminals with a powerful human body honed by intense exercise and a brilliant mind that uses scientific methods to solve crimes and create weapons like the batarang, a throwing device.

Batman had another powerful weapon against criminals—they feared him because of his intimidating presence. Bob Kane drew Batman as a menacing, mysterious figure, from the cowl with pointed ears that concealed his face to his flowing cape. Kane gave him one more frightening, mysterious feature

Bob Kane, who created the character of Batman in 1939, poses with several of his illustrations in 1966.

by making the eye holes of his mask blank to hide his emotions. Feiffer writes, "If that didn't strike terror into the hearts of evildoers, nothing would."[77] The world Batman inhabited was terrifying as well, filled with shadows and dark areas that made it easy to believe that danger lurked everywhere. Feiffer claims, "Batman inhabited a world where no one, no matter the time of day, cast anything but long shadows [because] Batman's world was scary."[78]

By 1941 fans were buying eight hundred thousand Batman comics each month. The commercial success of the first two superheroes led to a flood of copycats, like Wonder Man, who debuted in *Wonder Comics* the same month Batman did. The character created by Eisner wore a cape-less red costume and got his powers from a magic ring instead of being born on the planet Krypton like Superman. But Eisner was ordered to cease publication of Wonder Man after a court ruled the character was so similar to Superman that he violated fiction copyright laws.

Captain Marvel, who wore a red costume with a short white cape and a yellow lightning bolt on his chest, was another Superman clone that debuted in 1939. Billy Batson was a homeless newsboy of twelve who, by uttering the magic word "Shazzam," was transformed into an imposing adult figure who called himself Captain Marvel. He could fly and had other powers as well. For a few years Captain Marvel was even more popular than Superman. Comic art historian Dennis Gifford credits much of that success to the way he was drawn: "C.C. [Charles Clarence] Beck was the cartoonist who fashioned the captain and whose simple, clean, and mildly humorous style made him so popular with younger fans."[79] During the 1940s people bought more Captain Marvel than Superman comic books. But like Wonder Man, Captain Marvel's days ended in 1951 when a court ruled Beck had infringed on the copyright of Superman's character.

Despite such legal setbacks, comic books were overrun from 1938 to 1954 by more than seven hundred superheroes, all of them clad in tight-fitting costumes like the one Shuster created for Superman. Most had special powers of some kind: The Flash was incredibly fast; Green Lantern had a magic lantern that powered a ring he wore that allowed him to conjure any weapon or tool he needed; Sub-Mariner and Aquaman controlled sea creatures, could breathe underwater, and swim with superhuman speed; and the Human Torch could burst into flame and manipulate fire. Others were like Batman—humans who had trained themselves to perform impossible feats and fight crime, like Green Arrow, who used a bow and arrow.

One of the most unusual superheroes was Plastic Man, who could stretch his body into any form imaginable. Harvey writes that cartoonist Jack Cole "drew in a realistic if simplistic style"[80] and that his real artistry was in how he imaginatively used his character's power of elasticity to fight crime. When chasing crooks, Plastic Man's legs would stretch to impossible lengths so he could run fast. He could mold himself into any shape, even a carpet, to hide from criminals.

The superhero club gained its first female member when Wonder Woman arrived in the December 1941 issue of *All Star Comics*. A warrior princess of the Amazons of Greek mythology, she had superhuman strength, speed, and agility. William Moulton Marston, a psychologist who invented the polygraph machine, created her and wrote scripts for stories, and cartoonist Harry G. Peter drew her. Clad in a tight-fitting red top, short skirt, red boots, and a gold diadem (headband), Wonder Woman was a sexy comic heroine. But Sheldon Mayer, who edited the comic, says Marston envisioned her as a figure of female strength and independence, and he claims that "Marston was an early feminist."[81]

A female superhero was one of the many new ideas artists created to make comic books more interesting. Jerry Robinson helped Bob Kane draw Batman. He says artists were able to do whatever they wanted because "we didn't have traditions or too many taboos. [Comic book style] didn't have any past."[82] Within this new, experimental genre, the greatest comic book innovator was Will Eisner.

A Comic Book Genius

On June 2, 1940, Eisner's *The Spirit* debuted as a weekly comic book supplement in newspapers. His hero was Denny Colt, a former police detective who disguised himself with a blue mask to fight crime. Eisner wrote and drew the comic and was legendary for his artistry. His characters were drawn boldly and powerfully; the expressions on their faces were clear-cut and effortlessly conveyed emotion. Feiffer writes that Eisner was able to imbue his drawings with a solid reality like no one else: "Eisner's line had weight. Clothing sat on his characters heavily; when they bent an arm, deep folds sprang into action everywhere. When one Eisner character slugged another, a real fist hit real flesh. Violence was no externalized plot exercise, it was the gut of his style. Massive and indigestible, it curdled, lava-like, from the page."[83]

Eisner's use of color made his work even more interesting—some panels that are nearly all black to indicate darkness are lit in the center by bright yellow to highlight action. Most importantly, his inventive layouts and graphics expanded the creative boundaries of the new art form. This is how Harvey sums up Eisner's contributions to developing comic book art: "[No] one of Eisner's generation pushed against the envelope of possibilities harder or experimented as thoughtfully or skillfully over as long a period. And very few of his generation—or of any other—have had as much impact upon the medium as he."[84]

Most comic books had six or eight panels of the same size and shape on each page. Eisner ignored that standard as he configured them instead to tell stories more dramatically. In a February 13, 1949, story titled *Visitor*, he began one page with a full-length vertical column on the left that showed the Spirit standing at the rear of a menacing alley flanked by buildings. The thin, tall panel gave readers a sense of the height of the buildings and the alley's confined space. Eight more panels of varying sizes completed the page. The opposite page had narrative in red letters on a black background running down the left-hand side, while to the right was a visually stunning montage of six irregularly shaped panels, some in black-and-white and some in color.

Eisner was also artistic in how he framed his panels and the perspective he provided by varying long and close-up views. He was at his most inventive in *The Killer* on December 6,

Will Eisner, creator of the Spirit in 1940, works at his drawing table in 1998. Eisner's skillful drawings, use of color, and innovative storytelling, greatly influenced comics as an art form.

1948, when readers witnessed a murder through the eyes of a killer. In several panels, Eisner surrounded the action with two ovals representing the killer's eyes—eyelashes were visible to heighten the effect of the killer's eyes. In the panel in which the killer shoots, readers see only the frightened victim, the top of a gun barrel, white smoke, and the word "BANG!"[85]

For most of the twentieth century, blacks in comic books were either bit characters in jungle stories or portrayed as stereotypes that demeaned African Americans. Ebony White in Will Eisner's *The Spirit* talked in uneducated black dialect and was funny mainly because he was ignorant and superstitious. But in June 1947 Orrin Cromwell Evans and other black writers and cartoonists published *All-Negro Comics*. Evans wanted to present positive African American images because there were none in other comics. The forty-eight-page comic had heroic characters like Lion Man and detective Ace Harlem. Evans boasts in a foreword to the comic that "every brush stroke and pen line in the drawings on these pages are by Negro artists" and that it was "jam-packed with fast action, African adventure, good clean humor and fantasy."

Despite making history, this was the only issue of the comic. In May 1949 Jackie Robinson, the player who integrated baseball, got his own comic book, and in 1950 *Joe Louis Comics* starred the former heavyweight champion. In 1965 *Lobo* featured a gun-toting black Western hero, but it lasted only two issues.

Quoted in Tom Christopher. "Orrin C. Evans and the Story of All Negro Comics." www.tomchristopher.com/?op=home/Comic%20History/Orrin%20C.%20Evans%20and%20The%20Story%20of%20All%20Negro%20ComicsOrri.

Eisner is hailed as the most creative early comic book artist, but many others also influenced development of the new art form. Two of the most important were Joe Simon and Jack Kirby.

Captain America

Steve Rogers was a frail patriot who wanted to be a soldier so badly that he volunteered to test a dangerous experimental serum that would boost his physical abilities to their maximum. It transformed him into Captain America, one of the most beloved superheroes of the 1940s. Writer Joe Simon and artist Jack Kirby created the ultimate soldier in 1940, a year before the United States entered World War II. Kirby explains that the catalyst for their fictional hero was that the nation was on the verge of fighting Germany and Japan: "That's why Captain America was born. America needed a superpatriot."[86]

Kirby drew Captain America as the living embodiment of patriotic fervor. His costume was red, white, and blue, and he carried a triangular shield—the shape of his shield was later changed to round—that was blue with white and red stripes and white stars like the U.S. flag. The flag motif extended to the giant white star emblazoned on his chest and the red and white stripes beneath it. He wore calf-high red boots, and the hood covering his head featured the letter *A* with small wings near his ears to denote his incredible speed.

Other superheroes fought Germany and Japan in the comics, but Captain America was the most heroic—on the cover of the first issue of *Captain America* in March 1941, he is punching Nazi dictator Adolf Hitler. That cover displayed Kirby's unerring eye for drawing complex action involving multiple characters. The center of the cover features the captain punching Hitler. But a German soldier in the foreground has fired a pistol—the bullet is seen ricocheting off Captain America's shield—and in the background two other soldiers are aiming at Captain America, a third has fired another gun at him, and a fourth is monitoring a big screen that shows a German spy blowing up a supply of U.S. ammunition. Kirby's ability to draw exciting and detailed action resulted in awe-inspiring fight scenes. Kirby once said: "When Captain America got into a fight with a dozen guys he could lick those guys, and anybody who read the book could see how he did it. I'd arrange it so that a wonderful fight scene would come out almost like a ballet, and it wouldn't be the kind of fight that we'd ordinarily see [in comics]."[87]

Kirby's battle ballets even crossed panels. When Captain America hit someone, they would go flying into the next

Superheroes support the war effort against Japan and Germany by urging Americans to buy bonds and stamps on the cover of *World's Finest Comics* during World War II.

panel. The creative energy the writing-drawing duo brought to superhero comics made the genre even more popular. But although superheroes dominated the early decades of comic books, there were hundreds of other comic books in a wide variety of genres.

Scrooge McDuck

Some of the best-selling humor comics featured animal characters, many of them already famous because they starred in animated cartoons. In 1941 Mickey Mouse and Donald Duck began appearing in *Walt Disney's Comics and Stories*. Other cartoon stars in comic books include Bugs Bunny, Porky Pig, Daffy Duck, Woody Woodpecker, Andy Panda, and Felix the Cat. But only one person who drew animal characters is considered a great comic book artist—Carl Barks, the creator of Uncle Scrooge, one of the most beloved figures in comic book history.

Barks introduced Scrooge McDuck in 1947 in a Donald Duck story titled *Christmas on Bear Mountain*. Scrooge was Donald's fabulously wealthy but miserly uncle. Barks borrowed his first name from Ebenezer Scrooge, the lead character in the Charles Dickens classic *A Christmas Carol*. Uncle Scrooge was such a hit with fans that he soon got his

A FEMALE COMIC ARTIST

Lily Renée Phillips was one of the few female artists in the early decades of comic books. Born in Vienna, Austria, in 1925, she and her family fled to the United States in 1941 to escape Nazi persecution of Jews. In New York, Phillips began working in 1942 for Fiction House, which was known for comics starring female heroines like Sheena, a Tarzan-like character nicknamed Queen of the Jungle. The comics she worked on included *Senorita Rio*, *The Werewolf Hunter*, and *Jane Martin*. Ironically, the young woman who had to flee Nazi terror was able to fight them through comic book characters like Senorita Rio, an American secret agent who posed as a Brazilian entertainer to hunt down enemy agents. Comic historian Jim Amash has praised her work, saying, "Some people are just illustrators and some people are storytellers. She was actually both." She signed her work "L. Renée," and few knew she was a woman cartoonist. In 2011 female cartoonist and historian Trina Robbins published *Lily Renée, Escape Artist: From Holocaust Survivor to Comic Book Pioneer*, a graphic novel about her life.

Quoted in Adriane Quinlan. "A Real-Life Comic Book Superhero." *Newsweek*, August 9, 2010, p. 48.

own comic book. Unlike most comic book artists, Barks had complete control over his work because he also wrote scripts for his stories. Barks used that creative freedom to invent a unique comic universe centered in Duckburg, where Donald also lived. He then populated it with memorable characters like Gyro Gearloose, a chicken who invented brilliant but strange machines, and the Beagle Boys, a family of criminals who kept trying to steal Scrooge's wealth.

Because Scrooge did not trust banks, he kept his money in a huge, heavily fortified building. Some of the most memorable scenes Barks penned had Scrooge diving, over and over again like a porpoise, into a huge lake of paper money and coins to show how much he loved his wealth. Those scenes made fans wonder how much money Scrooge had. Barks once answered that question by estimating Scrooge's fortune with a made-up number— he said Scrooge had "one multiplujillion, nine obsquatumatillion, six hundred twenty-three dollars and sixty-two cents."[88]

Many of Scrooge's adventures took place in exotic locales around the world. Sharing those adventures were Donald and Donald's nephews Huey, Dewey, and Louie, whom Barks also created. The stories Barks wrote and drew were full of danger and thrilling adventures, some of which took up the entire comic book. Goulart writes that "[in] the full-length books he created [early] graphic novels that were full of adventure, satire, and some of the best cartooning to be found in comics."[89] Although Barks's drawing was memorable, his true artistry was how he structured panels to tell stories. Famed film director George Lucas, who created the *Star Wars* and *Indiana Jones* movies, read *Uncle Scrooge* comics while growing up. Lucas's love of Barks is evident in the film *Raiders of the Lost Ark* (1981) when Indiana Jones outraces a boulder rolling down a tunnel to avoid being crushed. The scene was borrowed from the *Uncle Scrooge* story "The Seven Cities of Cibola." In a foreword to a collection of Uncle Scrooge stories, Lucas writes: "[They] are very cinematic. They have a clear beginning, middle, and end, and operate in scenes, unlike many comic strips and books. Barks's stories don't just move from panel to panel,

Although some artists like Carl Barks did all the writing and drawing in their comic books, teams of artists working together in an assembly-line process produced most comic books. Writers created stories for comic books, including action sequences. Pencilers then used lead pencils to sketch the action in each panel, usually on a board measuring 11 by 17 inches (27.9cm by 43.2cm). This is one of the most important jobs, because the penciler not only created the basic artwork but also determined the flow and pacing of the action, which is key to telling the story. The pencil drawing then went to an inker, who went over the pencil lines to make them bolder for the printing process. The inker also shaded the drawing to give it depth and create moods. The writer used the pencil drawing to write dialogue, narrative, or sound effects to complete the story. A letterer wrote the dialogue boxes and sound effects the writer had created. The panels then went to a colorist, who colored the previously black-and-white images. This basic process is still used today to create comic books, although computers are used to provide more vivid coloring.

An art board shows a comic book page while it is still a work in progress.

A boy checks out the many comic book offerings at a drug store in 1956. Although many of the kid-oriented comics introduced in the 1940s and 1950s were not as artful as those that featured superheroes, they were nevertheless popular among young readers.

but flow in sequences—sometimes several pages long—that lead to new sequences."[90]

Most comic books were not as artistically done as *Uncle Scrooge*. Despite a relative lack of quality drawing and writing, scores of comics in the 1940s and 1950s were successful. There were comic books about Westerns, detectives, and outer space. Many comic books like *Little Lulu* and *Richie Rich* featured youngsters, while others like *Archie* featured teenage characters. In the 1950s the new medium of television spawned comic books featuring characters in popular shows, such as Howdy Doody, the puppet star of a children's program. And in 1941 *Classic Comics*—the name later became *Classics Illustrated*—tried to educate youngsters with comic book versions of classic novels like *The Three Musketeers*.

Many of those types of comic books were aimed at youngsters. Because of that, their stories and the quality of their art were usually not as good as superhero comics, which were also popular with adults. However, whatever their visual quality, the appeal of comics to readers of different ages and backgrounds made them an incredibly popular art form. And while some are more artistic than others, Goulart does not believe comic books have to be artistic to be entertaining. In his *Great History of Comic Books*, Goulart says that as a child, long before he learned the nuances of sequential art, he loved comic books because reading them made him happy. "There was an excitement to the work and feeling of fun," Goulart writes. "There was compelling movement, color, and, more frequently than might be expected, pretty good dialogue. [I] did know that I liked to read comic books and, often, just look at the pictures."[91] And that, Goulart claims, was enough to justify their existence.

5

Comic Art Evolves

Comic art has changed in many ways since the middle of the twentieth century, when comics were at the height of their popularity. Computers and the Internet have dramatically changed how artists create and publish their work. The artists themselves have changed, too. Comic artists are a more diverse group, with many more women artists as well as members of ethnic and racial minorities creating comic art than in previous decades. As the world has changed, so have the images and the messages being conveyed through comic art. One thing that has not changed is the main reason for creating such art, which is to tell a good story, to entertain or provoke, or to comment on events of national or global importance.

Artists are often inspired to memorialize or comment on important historical events. In 1937, Picasso painted *Guernica* when German and Italian warplanes bombed Spanish soldiers and civilians during the Spanish Civil War. The mural-sized oil painting—11.5 feet (3.5m) tall by 25.6 feet (7.8m) wide— protested this new, savage type of warfare with an abstract montage of body parts from animals and people that had been blown to bits. After the terrorist attacks on the United States on September 11, 2001, comic artists were likewise compelled to commemorate the most deadly attacks ever on U.S. soil. Library of Congress art curator Martha Kennedy explains what motivated them: "Some cartoonists stated that when they could find no direct means of aiding those in need, they turned to creative expression as the only way to react constructively. [The] arresting union of form and meaning that distinguishes this artistic mode from others, enabled these artists to respond to 9/11 with immediacy and ingenuity."[92]

Every newspaper and magazine printed editorial cartoons after the attacks, and many cartoonists also expressed themselves through their art. Will Eisner's *Reality 9/11* is a haunting vision in shades of gray of a man watching television as the Twin Towers of New York's World Trade Center collapse after being rammed by two airplanes. The seated man is covered with ashes that blew out of the television set's shattered screen, while above him floats smoke that drifted out of the set from the horrific scene. A stream of red representing blood from victims—the only bright color in the one-panel cartoon—leaks out of the television. Eisner once claimed that comic art "enables people to talk with images"[93]—his message that the attacks affected every American needed no words.

Other cartoonists also referenced the attacks in their drawings. On December 23, 2001, Garry Trudeau's Sunday *Doonesbury* strip featured the characters Zonker Harris and B.D. standing before the ruins of the Twin Towers, now blanketed by snow. Zonker, a peace-loving hippie, yells, "Peace out, dawg!" while the helmeted soldier replies, "Same back atcha, citizen!"[94] The attacks united them even though they have different philosophical perspectives. In another example, comic book artist Alex Ross drew a stunning scene in which Superman and Krypto, his super dog, are gazing at a mural high above them depicting firemen, policemen, and other emergency personnel who helped victims of the attacks. The giant mural dwarfs the super-powered duo, and Ross's message is easily understood—emergency personnel, not comic book superheroes, are the real heroes.

Those comic artists were doing what their predecessors had been doing for centuries. Yet by the twenty-first century,

The Far Side

From January 1, 1980, until January 1, 1995, Gary Larson drew some of the strangest but funniest one-panel cartoons ever to grace the newspaper comic page. *The Far Side* was distributed to nineteen hundred newspapers and translated into seventeen languages. His fans have bought tens of thousands of book-length collections of his whimsical cartoons and more than 3 million *Far Side* calendars. Larson once wrote, "The goal in any cartoon is to create that perfect marriage between the drawing and the caption (if there is one)." Larson's cartoons were well drawn, but his real artistry was his diabolical sense of humor, which led to impossibly weird images. In *Sled Chickens of the North*, chickens are pulling a sled through snow. In a wordless cartoon, two taxis are speeding through a forest—the passenger in the first is a sheep who is being pursued by a wolf in the second. Larson loved snakes; one cartoon featured snakes sitting in a restaurant trying to decide whether to order a hamster or a rat for dinner.

Gary Larson. *The PreHistory of "The Far Side": A 10th Anniversary Exhibit*. Kansas City, MO: Andrews and McMeel, 1990, p. 141.

the comic art they and other artists were producing had been transformed in many ways.

New Types of Comic Strips

One of the biggest changes in comic strips since the middle of the twentieth century is the increased diversity both of the characters and of the cartoonists. Brumsic Brandon Jr. was born April 10, 1927, in Washington, D.C. Brandon says that as a child he hated the way blacks were portrayed in comic strips: "During my youth there were very few black characters on comic pages of the nation's mainstream [white] newspapers and the ones that were there were detestable. Without dwelling on the degrading details, animal characters were assigned more human qualities than were black people."[95]

Brandon began drawing cartoons and comic strips to counter racial stereotypes with positive black images. In 1966 *Luther*, his strip about a young black boy, debuted in newspapers. For the next two decades, Brandon commented on race through characters he created who lived in a poor black neighborhood. Ray Billingsley is one of many black cartoonists to come on the scene since then. Billingsley's *Curtis* began in 1988 and features Curtis Wilkins, a young boy with a tall Afro who is always getting into trouble. The strip has an enduring theme of black pride. Each year Billingsley tells an African-themed tale during Kwanzaa, the period from December 26 to January 1 in which African Americans celebrate their heritage. Newer comic strips like *Curtis* and *Boondocks* that feature African Americans no longer dwell primarily on the injustice of racial discrimination. The newer strips are about family life and other more universal topics as well.

One of the earliest comic strips to feature Hispanic characters and experiences was *Gordo*, drawn by Gustavo "Gus" Arriola. The strip was about a bean farmer named Perfecto Salazar. It ran in syndication from November 24, 1941, to March 2, 1985. *Peanuts* creator Charles Schulz once said *Gordo* was "probably the most beautifully drawn strip in the history of the business."[96] Arriola's artistry made his characters come to life. He also used shadows effectively to create moods and different perspectives in his cartoon panels. Comic historian Robert C. Harvey claims *Gordo* educated non-Hispanics about Hispanic culture and introduced them to Spanish words like *amigo* and *piñata*. *Baldo*, written by Hector Cantú and drawn by Carlos Castellanos, began in April 2000. Cantú and Castellanos have used the strip about high school student Baldomero Bermudez and his family to update the image of Hispanics and comment on immigration and other issues important to Hispanics.

Such political commentary is something that has been featured in comic strips for a long time. On October 4, 1948, Walt Kelly began *Pogo*, which starred a philosophical possum who lived in Georgia's Okefenokee Swamp. Pogo and

other characters like cigar-smoking Albert Alligator had been
around since 1941 in *Pogo* comic books. When a New York
newspaper hired Kelly to draw political cartoons, he decided
to use his animal characters to comment on politics. Comic
historian Harry Katz writes that "Kelly was the first modern
cartoonist to introduce explicit and specific political caricature
into a national syndicated comic strip."[97] Until the strip ended

July 20, 1975, Kelly made people laugh and think seriously about political figures and issues.

Kelly was the inspiration for other politically oriented strips as well. The best was *Doonesbury*, a strip about college students that began on October 26, 1970. Just five years later, Garry Trudeau won a Pulitzer Prize for his biting, satiric commentary on political and social issues. Trudeau's humor was sharper and harder-hitting than that of Kelly's. He also aimed his cartoon barbs directly at political figures he disagreed with, like Presidents Richard Nixon and George W. Bush, instead of creating humorous animals who symbolized political figures.

In 2003 Darrin Bell started *Candorville*. The cartoon strip comments on political and social issues through the lives of black and Latino characters who live in the inner city, like Lemont Brown, a struggling writer who works at Pigville Pork Burgers, and his best friend Susan Garcia, an advertising executive. In an interview, Bell once said he is more concerned about commenting on issues than making people laugh: "So I don't try to be funny, I just try to speak my truth and hope other people relate to it."[98] In 2012 Bell used his characters to comment from a liberal point of view on topics like the Republican presidential primary race and the death of Trayvon Martin, a Florida teenager shot to death by a community watch coordinator, which raised questions about racist stereotypes and treatment of blacks. A comic strip that comments on politics from the conservative point of view was started in 1994 by Bruce Tinsley. In his strip, called *Mallard Fillmore*, the title character is a duck who is a television reporter—his name is a pun on Millard Fillmore, the thirteenth U.S. president.

While political cartoonists may be more interested in making their readers think instead of laugh, humor has continued to play a significant role in comics. For a time, humor was about all that could be found on the comics page.

Peanuts Changes Comic Strips

The adventure strips that dominated comic pages through the 1940s began to fade away in the second half of the twentieth century. Harvey claims that Charles Schulz was responsible for the change. Schulz's *Peanuts* debuted on October 2, 1950, and ran until February 13, 2000; reprints of it still appear in newspapers today. *Peanuts* is one of the most beloved strips of all time, and characters like Charlie Brown and his dog, Snoopy, are known the world over. Harvey claims, "Schulz began a revolution in 1950 with his simply drawn strip and [its success] demonstrated to the satisfaction of most newspaper editors and [comic strip] syndicates that the reading public wanted a laugh-a-day type of comic strip."[99] In the next few decades, newspapers began dropping adventure strips that told stories over several weeks for humor strips. There was also a decline in continuity in humor strips; more artists began writing strips that ended with a funny punch line in the final panel each day, instead of creating humorous situations that extended over several days or even weeks.

Schulz also brought a new style of art to comic strips. This is how comic historian John Carlin describes Schulz's artwork: "From the start [his] drawings were pure and simple. [He] is able to give a sense of what is happening through a bare minimum of lines."[100] Panels in *Peanuts* have lots of space, his characters are simply drawn, and his backgrounds are unadorned. One reason that other cartoonists copied Schulz's bare-bones style is that the space newspapers devoted to comic strips had been shrinking for several decades.

Daily comic strips before World War II were often 10.25 inches (26cm) long and 3 inches (7.6cm) high. When newspapers began conserving paper for the war effort, they reduced strips to 7.5 inches (19cm) to 2.5 inches (6.4cm). In the decades following the war, strip sizes grew even smaller as newspapers reduced page sizes to cut costs. By 2012 daily strips in some papers measured only 5 inches (12.7cm) long by 1.75 inches (4.4cm) high. Sunday comic strips that once took up full pages were also drastically reduced during that period.

Harvey claims that smaller panels degraded the quality of comic strip art. He also believes the decreased size helped kill most adventure strips, which require more elaborately drawn figures and backgrounds to tell complex, ongoing stories than humor strips. Harvey writes: "Serious storytelling strips felt the

Charles Schulz draws a *Peanuts* comic strip in the 1970s. *Peanuts* is considered one of the most beloved comic strips of all time.

pinch more than the gag-a-day strips. In such small panels, it was difficult to draw enough picture to produce the illusion of reality essential to making such narratives convincing and engrossing. [Without] space in which to illustrate, the visual rhetoric of the medium was seriously impaired."[101]

Smaller spaces, however, did not diminish the creativity of cartoonists, who are still finding imaginative new ways to make people laugh. One way they have done that is to draw strips that make it appear as if their characters are visiting other comic strips or that characters from other strips have traveled to their strips. In the *Mother Goose and Grimm* strip for February 2, 2012, Grimm, a bull terrier, digs in the ground of the first panel to get out of a fenced-in yard. When his head pops up in the next panel, which has characters from Lynn Johnston's comic strip *For Better or for Worse*, his eyes go wide as he realizes, "Uh-oh . . . I forgot! . . . they age in real time in that strip."[102] The final panel shows an ancient Grimm using a walker. Johnston is one of the few comic strip artists who allow their characters to grow older. Because comic strips are laid out side-by-side, such inter-strip visits seem natural.

Despite criticism that comic strip art has deteriorated, venerated comic strip artist Mort Walker believes they still fulfill an important function by making people laugh. He says of the comics page, "You have a spread of human experiences, zapped with a humorous spark, a smorgasbord of life. [What] a way to start the day! With a smile."[103] Walker should know—he began drawing *Beetle Bailey* in 1950 and *Hi and Lois* in 1954, and both were still being published today in 2012.

New Superheroes

The evolution of comic art has been even greater in comic books. At their peak in the late 1940s and early 1950s, nearly 1 billion comic books were sold annually. Sales declined after that and never reached such heights again. Some companies quit publishing comics, but superhero comics continued to sell well even though their prices rose. The 1960s was the last decade in which comics still cost a dime. By the early 1970s comic books were priced at twenty cents even though they had only thirty-two pages, only half the number of earlier comic books, and by 2012 they cost several dollars each.

Comic book publishers in the 1970s tried to sustain the popularity of superheroes by resurrecting old characters from the 1940s and creating new ones. In an attempt to create greater interest in its line of comics that featured Superman and Batman, DC Comics brought back 1940s characters the

Flash and Green Lantern. When the revivals proved successful, the company teamed up superheroes in the Justice League of America, whose star-studded roster included Superman, Batman, the Flash, Green Lantern, Aquaman, and Wonder Woman. The Justice League debuted in the March 1960 issue of *The Brave and the Bold*. Mike Sekowsky, who drew the superheroes, says, "It was a thrilling moment for DC's older fans."[104] Letters DC received showed that more adults were buying their comics, which meant the company was widening the audience for its comic books.

DC's success inspired writer Stan Lee and artist Jack Kirby to create new characters for Marvel Comics, which had abandoned the superhero genre after success in the 1940s with characters like Captain America. Their first effort was *The Fantastic Four*, and its first issue in November 1961 introduced a new breed of superhero. Lee explains why he created a different type of superhero: "The characters would be the kind of character I could personally relate to; they'd be flesh and blood, they'd have their faults and foibles, they'd be fallible and feisty,

Stan Lee created many superheroes for Marvel Comics, including Spider-Man, who was introduced in 1962.

and—most important of all—inside their colorful, costumed booties, they'd still have feet of clay."[105]

The four were Mr. Fantastic, who can stretch his body into any length or shape; Invisible Woman, who becomes invisible and projects force fields; Human Torch, who can fly and transform into flame that he can control; and Thing, a rough-hided, nearly invulnerable orange monstrosity with superhuman strength. They differed from other superheroes because they had no secret identities; they were astronauts who gained their superpowers by exposure to cosmic radiation on a space mission, which meant the world knew who they were. Also unlike comic rivals such as Superman, they had psychological and social problems like those of real people. Thing (Ben Grimm) was angry that he had been transformed into something hideous even though he had gained superpowers, and Mr. Fantastic, Reed Richards, mourned the loss of his quiet life as a scientist.

Lee and Kirby continued to create superheroes with great powers and difficult personal problems. The Incredible Hulk, introduced in May 1962, was a mindless green giant with incredible strength. Robert Bruce Banner, the mild-mannered scientist who became the Hulk whenever he got angry, agonized over the damage he caused as Hulk and how being Hulk had ruined his life. Spider-Man debuted in August 1962. Despite gaining superpowers from a radioactive spider, Peter Parker felt guilty that even with his special powers he had failed to save his uncle from being killed by a criminal. Spider-Man is Lee's greatest creation. Lee admits he broke a lot of comic book formulas in creating Spider-Man: "A strip that would actually feature a teenager as the star. A strip in which the main character would lose out as often as he'd win—in fact, more often."[106]

The unusual stories involving complex, conflicted heroes generated new interest in comic books. So did some of the art. In 1963 Marvel created the X-Men, a superhero team of mutants who were schooled by Professor Charles Francis Xavier, himself a mutant. Neal Adams was the artist for *The X-Men*. Comic book historian Ron Goulart says of Adams: "He had a sophisticated, bravura style. [When] it came to laying out a

*U*ncanny X-Men is a 1991 comic book that *Guinness World Records* recognized in 2010 as the best-selling ever because fans bought more than 8.1 million copies. The penciler for that record-setting comic was Jim Lee, who was born in Seoul, Korea, on August 11, 1964, but moved to St. Louis, Missouri, with his family when he was four. Lee was such a good artist at Saint Louis Country Day School that classmates predicted in his senior yearbook that he would one day own his own comic book company. Lee admits that his passion for art almost got him into trouble in grade school: "In third or fourth grade, a substitute teacher ripped a drawing out of my hand and was about to crumple it up and throw it away, but instead she got this look on her face like she liked it, and she hung it up in front of her desk." Lee began working for Marvel Comics after graduating from Princeton University and quickly became recognized as one of the industry's top artists.

Quoted in Byron Kerman. "Comic Genius." *St. Louis Magazine*, July 2010. www.stlmag.com/St-Louis-Magazine/July-2010/Comic-Genius.

Jim Lee draws Batman in 2003.

story, though, Adams was much more unconventional than the competition. His panels sliced pages up in unexpected ways, his long and medium shots favored unusual angles and perspectives, and his close-ups rarely showed his heroes striking a handsome pose. The work was both slick and gritty."[107]

The trend to more adult themes in superhero comics coincided with another step in the evolution of sequential art—the graphic novel. Once again, legendary artist Will Eisner helped pioneer this new comic art format.

Graphic Novels and Manga

Eisner's 1978 *A Contract with God, and Other Tenement Stories* is generally considered the first graphic novel. Eisner used four semiautobiographical stories about his childhood in the Bronx, New York, in the 1930s to focus on man's relationship with God. Eisner used the term for the new comic art when he telephoned a book publisher about buying his book, as he explains: "A little man in my head popped up and said, 'For Christ's sake stupid, don't tell him it's a comic. He'll hang up on you.' So, I said, 'It's a graphic novel.' He said, 'Wow! That sounds interesting. Come on up.'"[108] The publisher rejected the work, but Eisner found a company to print it. Eisner was neither the first person to use the term *graphic novel* nor the first to create book-length sequential art, but his comic art fame helped popularize both the term and new format.

Graphic novels today consist of lengthy sequential art that can either entertain people with stories about characters like Superman or deal with serious subjects such as the Holocaust. An example of the latter type of graphic novel is *Maus: A Survivor's Tale*, in which Art Spiegelman tells the story of his father, a survivor of a German concentration camp. Holocaust historian Robert S. Leventhal writes that "*Maus* is the use of a traditionally 'low' genre—the comic strip or book—for serious, grave material."[109] *Maus* was so moving that Spiegelman received a 1991 Pulitzer Prize Special Award for Literature, even though judges admitted they did not know exactly what kind of literary work it was. In addition, graphic novels are often appreciated as much for the artistry of their drawings as for the stories they tell.

Similar to graphic novels are manga, Japanese sequential art. Manga—the Japanese word for "comics"—is a descendant of Japanese cartoons and comic strips. The Japanese artists who began producing manga after World War II were influenced by comic books U.S. soldiers introduced to Japan. In the 1950s Osamu Tezuka created *Astro Boy*, a robot from a future in which humans and robots live together. Manga were extremely popular because of cute characters and humor, but Tezuka tried to make *Astro Boy* more than a series of funny stories. In his autobiography, Tezuka writes that "comics were capable of more than just making people laugh [so] in my themes I incorporated tears, grief, anger and hate, and I created stories where the ending was not always 'happy.'"[110] Other

A mural of Astro Boy in Tokyo, Japan. Osamu Tezuka's *Astro Boy*, which debuted in the 1950s, is an iconic example of Japanese manga.

Comic art has a prominent place in cyberspace. Comic strips can be read on Internet sites as well as in newspapers, and publishers sell digital comic books for a fraction of the cost of a paper-and-ink version. Even more exciting, various types of comic art known as webcomics, online comics, or Internet comics are being published exclusively on the Internet. Internet comics debuted in 1985 with Eric Millikin's *Witches and Stitches*, a comic book parody of the *Wizard of Oz*. The first comic strip published online six years later was Hans Bjordahl's *Where the Buffalo Roam*. Webcomic artists have shown new creativity in their work but have not made a major impact on comic art. Bart Beaty is head of the University of Calgary English Department and a comic art historian. He said in 2011, "Few webcartoonists have been able to make a huge impact outside the world of webcomics. It still remains this small, very marginal niche."

Quoted in Sarah Dorchak. "Pioneering the Page: The Decline of Print Comics, the Growth of Webcomics and the Flexibility, Innovation and Controversy of Both." *Gauntlet*, September 29, 2011. http://thegauntlet .ca/story/15763?qt=CJSW%20faces%20changing%20tides.

Japanese artists also began producing more literary works, like *Lone Wolf and Cub*, an influential series about a samurai warrior and his young son set in medieval Japan. Interestingly, it was a Japanese manga that had a profound effect on the way comic art looks today.

The Digital Comic Age

Comic artists still use pencils to draw figures and background for cartoons, comic strips, and comic books, but most now use computers to add more vivid color to their work. Bob Thaves began drawing the comic strip *Frank & Ernest* in 1972. The digital company Electric Crayon began coloring his Sunday strips in 1995. Thaves says after that, one fan sent him an e-mail gushing about the "amazing color" the strip now had, and another noted that the strip now "jump(s) off the page."[111]

Coloring pages using computer tools and techniques has been even more important in comic books because every page is colored. Steve Oliff helped pioneer digital coloring in *Akira*, a 1987 Marvel version of the popular Japanese manga by Katsuhiro Otomo. He had been experimenting for a while with using computer programs to color when Marvel editors asked him to send four sample computer-colored pages of *Akira*. Oliff says, "Comics in Japan are black and white, but for the English translation they wanted it to be in color. I'd never heard of *Akira*, but I decided to pull out all the stops on my color test."[112] The pages looked so good that Marvel let his firm, Olyoptics, color the comic.

Since then Oliff has won many industry awards for coloring comic books featuring characters like Batman and Spawn. More importantly, computer coloring looked so good that Oliff's work changed the way most comic books are colored. Other publishers began using digital coloring, and by 2007 Oliff could proudly say, "These days comics are colored on computers."[113] Publishers switched because digital coloring created a vibrant new look that made the finished work resemble a painting more than something drawn and colored by hand.

Dave McCaig has used computers to color high-profile comics like *Superman: Birthright*, a twelve-comic series in 2003 and 2004 that updated the original superhero for the twenty-first century. This is how McCaig explains his job as a colorist: "Colorists are the cinematographers of the comic industry. We are not responsible for telling the story in as direct a way as the writer or penciller is, but [we] set the tone and mood with color, we direct your eye across the page, and set up depth of field."[114]

To further heighten the effect of digital coloring, most comic books are now printed on coated paper instead of cheap pulp paper as in the past. Layouts and drawings in comic books are also more interesting today because pencilers have become more daring in structuring panels and more creative in depicting characters and scenes.

Comic Art's Future

Changes in various types of comic art since the 1950s have generally enhanced them and upgraded their image in the art world. Will Eisner had always hated that his work and that of other comic artists was never considered art and that most people thought it was only something to amuse children. But in a speech in 2002 to comic artists and historians, Eisner said the future of comic art was bright because it was finally being taken seriously: "This [is] a moment in time for which I have been dreaming all of my professional life. [Comic art is] now being discussed as a form of literature, and this is what I've been hoping for in all these years."[115] Eisner died three years later, on January 3, 2005, fully confident that the much-maligned art form he had helped create would continue to flourish in the future.

A comic book artist uses a digital pen and a special display monitor to create her work. Computer tools and techniques are regularly used to draw and color comics.

Notes

Introduction: A Powerful New Art Form

1. Will Eisner. "Getting the Last Laugh: My Life in Comics." *New York Times Book Review*, January 14, 1990, p. 1.

2. Robert C. Harvey. *The Art of the Comic Book: An Aesthetic History.* Jackson: University Press of Mississippi, 1996, p. 18.

3. Bill Blackbeard and Martin Williams, eds. *The Smithsonian Collection of Newspaper Comics.* Washington, DC: Smithsonian Institution, 1977, p. 13.

4. Quoted in Roger Sabin. *Comics, Comix & Graphic Novels: A History of Comic Art.* London: Phaidon, 1996, p. 9.

5. Harry Katz, ed. *Cartoon America: Comic Art in the Library of Congress.* New York: Abrams, 2006, p. 307.

6. Jules Feiffer. *The Great Comic Book Heroes.* Seattle: Fantagraphics, 2003, p. 73.

Chapter 1: A History of Comic Art

7. Scott Adams. *Dilbert. Milwaukee Journal-Sentinel*, October 20, 2011, p. D2.

8. Quoted in Brian Walker. *The Comics: The Complete Collection.* New York: Abrams, 2008, p. 13.

9. Will Eisner. *Graphic Storytelling and Visual Narrative.* New York: Norton, 2008, p. 1.

10. Syd Hoff. *Editorial and Political Cartooning.* New York: Stravon Educational Press, 1976, p. 30.

11. Mark Bryant, "The First American Political Cartoon." *History Today,* December 2007, p. 58.

12. Quoted in Stephen Becker. *Comic Art in America.* New York: Simon and Schuster, 1959, p. 14.

13. Becker. *Comic Art in America*, p. 13.

14. Will Eisner. *Graphic Storytelling and Visual Narrative.* Tamarac, FL: Poorhouse, 1996, p. 6.

15. Richard F. Outcault. *R.F. Outcault's the Yellow Kid: A Centennial Celebration of the Kid Who Started the Comics.* Northampton, MA: Kitchen Sink, 1995, plate 42.

16. Robert C. Harvey. *Children of the Yellow Kid.* Seattle: Frye Art Museum, 1998, p. 20.

17. Sabin. *Comics, Comix & Graphic Novels*, p. 20.
18. Quoted in Harvey. *The Art of the Comic Book*, p. 18.
19. Quoted in Les Daniels. *DC Comics: A Celebration of the World's Most Favorite Comic Book Heroes*. New York: Billboard, 1995, p. 21.
20. Dennis Gifford. *The International Book of Comics*. New York: Crescent, 1984, p. 114.
21. Becker. *Comic Art in America*, p. 13.

Chapter 2: Single-Panel Cartoons

22. Syd Hoff. "About Syd Hoff: Autobiography." Syd Hoff: Cartoonist & Author. http://sydhoff.org.
23. Quoted in Michael Cavna. "Timeless Syd Hoff: How a Depression-Era Cartoonist Speaks to the Occupy Movement." *Washington Post*, November 2, 2011. www.washingtonpost.com/blogs/comic-riffs/post/timeless-syd-hoff-how-a-depression-era-cartoonist-speaks-to-the-occupy-movement/2011/11/02/gIQAitCGhM_blog.html.
24. Hoff. *Editorial and Political Cartooning*, p. 13.
25. Becker. *Comic Art in America*, p. 289.
26. Maurice Horn, ed. *World Encyclopedia of Cartoons*. New York: Chelsea House, 1980, p. 19.
27. Quoted in Phrase Finder. "The Pen Is Mightier than the Sword." www.phrases.org.uk/meanings/the-pen-is-mightier-than-the-sword.html.
28. Becker. *Comic Art in America*, p. 4.
29. Katz. *Cartoon America*, p. 28.
30. Quoted in Cartoon of the Day. "Compromise with the South." *HarpWeek* Cartoons. www.harpweek.com/09Cartoon/RelatedCartoon.asp?Month=September&Date=3.
31. Quoted in Dan Gilgoff. "Picture Power." *U.S. News & World Report*, March 20, 2008, p. 38.
32. Quoted in Morton Keller. "The World of Thomas Nast." Ohio State University. http://cartoons.osu.edu/nast/keller_web.htm.
33. Herbert Block. "Tsk Tsk—Somebody Should Do Something About That." Herblock's History: Political Cartoons from the Crash to the Millennium. www.loc.gov/rr/print/swann/herblock/presidents.html.
34. Quoted in Katz. *Cartoon America*, p. 252.
35. Quoted in Eric Pace. "Oliver Harrington, Cartoonist Who Created 'Bootsie,' Dies at 84." *New York Times*, November 7, 1995, p. 22.
36. Hoff. *Editorial and Political Cartooning*, p. 13.
37. Quoted in Katz. *Cartoon America*, p. 156.
38. Quoted in Edward Rothstein. "The Perverse Pleasures Underneath the Ordinary." *New York Times*, March 4, 2010. www.nytimes.com/2010/03/05/arts/design/05addams.html?pagewanted=all.
39. Quoted in Don Martin. *The Completely Mad Don Martin*. Philadelphia: Running Press, 2007, p. 3.

40. Quoted in Richard Gehr. "Gahan Wilson and the Comedy of the Weird." *Comics Journal*, April 27, 2011. www.tcj.com/gahan-wilson.

41. Thomas Nast, "The Third-Term Panic." HarpWeek.com. www.harpweek.com/09cartoon/browsebydatecartoon.asp?month=november&date=7 November 7, 1874.

42. Quoted in American Treasures of the Library of Congress. "The Most Famous Poster." www.loc.gov/exhibits/treasures/trm015.html.

43. Quoted in American Treasures of the Library of Congress. "The Most Famous Poster."

44. R.J. Brown. "Thomas Nast: The Power of One Person's Wood Engravings." HistoryBuff.com. www.historybuff.com/library/refnast.html.

45. Quoted in Edward Rothstein. "Is It Still a Mad, Mad, Mad, Mad World?" *New York Times*, September 18, 2009. http://topics.nytimes.com/topics/reference/timestopics/organizations/m/mad_magazine/index.html.

46. Quoted in Katz. *Cartoon America*, p. 7.

Chapter 3: Comic Strips

47. Quoted in Harvey. *Children of the Yellow Kid*, p. 10.

48. Quoted in John Carlin, Paul Karasik, and Brian Walker, eds. *Masters of American Comics*. New Haven, CT: Yale University Press, 2005, p. 42.

49. Quoted in Sarah Boxer. "Herriman: Cartoonist Who Equalled Cervantes." *Telegraph* (London), July 7, 2007. www.telegraph.co.uk/culture/books/3666365/Herriman-Cartoonist-who-equalled-Cervantes.html.

50. Gilbert Seldes. *The Seven Lively Arts*. New York: Harper, 1924, p. 231.

51. Eisner. *Graphic Storytelling and Visual Narrative*, 2008, p. xii.

52. Harvey. *Children of the Yellow Kid*, p. 27.

53. Becker. *Comic Art in America*, pp. 233–234.

54. Coulton Waugh. *The Comics*. New York: Luna, 1974, p. 20.

55. Patrick McDonnell. *Mutts. Milwaukee Journal Sentinel*, December 7, 2011, p. G10.

56. Richard Marschall. *America's Great Comic-Strip Artists: From the Yellow Kid to Peanuts*. New York: Stewart, Tabori and Chang, 1997, pp. 9–10.

57. Al Capp. *The World of Li'l Abner*. New York: Ballantine, 1965, p. xi.

58. Blackbeard and Williams. *The Smithsonian Collection of Newspaper Comics*, p. 16.

59. Becker. *Comic Art in America*, p. 13.

60. Quoted in Ron Goulart. *The Adventurous Decade*. New Rochelle, NY: Arlington House, 1975, p. 49.

61. Waugh. *The Comics*, p. 92.

62. Quoted in Harvey. *Children of the Yellow Kid*, p. 79.

63. Carlin et al. *Masters of American Comics*, p. 79.

64. Quoted in Katz. *Cartoon America*, p. 174.

65. Quoted in Marschall. *America's Great Comic-Strip Artists*, p. 173.

66. "Leapin' Lizards, It's the End for 'Annie.'" *New York Times,* May 14, 2010, p. 14.
67. Capp. *The World of Li'l Abner*, p. xi.
68. Marschall. *America's Great Comic-Strip Artists*, p. 254.
69. Walker. *The Comics*, p. 347.

Chapter 4: Comic Books

70. Eisner. "Getting the Last Laugh," p. 1.
71. Quoted in Daniels. *DC Comics*, p. 22.
72. Harvey. *The Art of the Comic Book*, p. 18.
73. Feiffer. *The Great Comic Book Heroes*, p. 13.
74. Ron Goulart. *The Great Comic Book Artists*. New York: St. Martin's, 1986, p. 94.
75. Feiffer. *The Great Comic Book Heroes*, p. 14.
76. Daniels. *DC Comics*, p. 28.
77. Feiffer. *The Great Comic Book Heroes*, p. 14.
78. Feiffer. *The Great Comic Book Heroes*, p. 28.
79. Gifford. *The International Book of Comics*, p. 122.
80. Harvey. *The Art of the Comic Book*, p. 21.
81. Quoted in Daniels. *DC Comics*, p. 58.
82. Quoted in Mike Benton. *The Illustrated History: Superhero Comics of the Golden Age*. Dallas: Taylor, 1992, p. 6.
83. Quoted in Ken Quattro. "Making of a Genius." Comicartville Library, 2003. www.comicartville.com/rareeisner.htm.
84. Harvey. *The Art of the Comic Book*, p. 66.
85. Will Eisner. *The Best of the Spirit*. New York: DC Comics, 2005, p. 52.
86. Quoted in Harvey. *The Art of the Comic Book*, p. 31.
87. Quoted in Benton. *The Illustrated History*, pp. 84–85.
88. Carl Barks, *Uncle Scrooge: His Life & Times*. Berkeley, CA: Celestial Arts, 1987, p. 7.
89. Goulart. *The Great Comic Book Artists*, p. 214.
90. Quoted in Carl Barks. *Uncle Scrooge*, p. 9.
91. Goulart. *The Great Comic Book Artists*, pp. v–vi.

Chapter 5: Comic Art Evolves

92. Quoted in Katz. *Cartoon America*, p. 300.
93. Quoted in Katz. *Cartoon America*, p. 300.
94. Garry Trudeau. "Doonesbury." December 23, 2011. GoComics. www.gocomics.com/doonesbury/2001/12/23.
95. Quoted in Katz. *Cartoon America*, p. 252.
96. Quoted in Hector Cantú. "Gordo Creator Took Accent off Stereotype." *Dallas Morning News*, December 11, 2000, p. 12.
97. Katz. *Cartoon America*, p. 10.
98. Quoted in Michael A. Ventrella. "Interview with Writer and Artist Darrin Bell." *Michael Ventrella's Blog*, September 14, 2011. http://michaelaventrella.wordpress.com/2011/09/14/interview-with-writer-and-artist-darrin-bell.

99. Harvey. *Children of the Yellow Kid*, p. 114.
100. Quoted in Carlin et al. *Masters of American Comics*, p. 88.
101. Harvey. *Children of the Yellow Kid*, p. 128.
102. Quoted in Mike Peters. *Mother Goose and Grimm. Milwaukee Journal Sentinel*, February 2, 2012, p. E2.
103. Quoted in Harvey. *Children of the Yellow Kid*, p. 9.
104. Quoted in Ron Goulart. *Ron Goulart's Great History of Comic Books.* Chicago: Contemporary Books, 1986, p. 281.
105. Stan Lee. *Origins of Marvel Comics.* New York: Simon and Schuster, 1974, p. 17.
106. Quoted in Goulart. *Ron Goulart's Great History of Comic Books*, p. 284.
107. Goulart. *The Great Comic Book Artists*, p. 2.
108. Will Eisner. "Keynote Address from the 2002 'Will Eisner Symposium.'" ImageTexT Interdisciplinary Comics Studies. www.english.ufl.edu/imagetext/archives/v1_1/eisner.
109. Robert S. Leventhal. "Art Spiegelman's *Maus*: Working-Through the Trauma of the Holocaust." University of Virginia, 1995. www2.iath.virginia.edu/holocaust/spiegelman.html.
110. Quoted in Jason Yadao. *The Rough Guide to Mangas.* London: Rough Guides, 2009, p. 13.
111. Quoted in *Editor & Publisher.* "Digital Color Is Now in 'Frank & Ernest,'" July 29, 1995, p. 33.
112. Steve Oliff. "Colouring the Akira Comics." Akira2019.com. www.akira2019.com/colouring-the-akira-manga.htm.
113. Quoted in Richard Vasseur. "Steve Oliff Colorist of Gumby." Jazma Online, September 22, 2007. www.jazmaonline.com/interviews/interviews2007.asp?intID=607.
114. Quoted in Arune Singh. "Dave McCaig Talks 'Superman' Birthright." Comic Book Resources, August 15, 2003. www.comicbookresources.com/?page=article&id=2611.
115. Eisner. "Keynote Address from the 2002 'Will Eisner Symposium.'"

Glossary

caricature: A type of cartoon that exaggerates the way people look to mock their ideas, personalities, or accomplishments.

cartoon: A drawing, usually coupled with words, designed to amuse, educate, or express a viewpoint.

cartoonist: An artist who draws comic art.

comic art: A term for cartoons, comic strips, comic books, and graphic novels.

comic artist: An artist who draws comic art.

comic strip (single panel or multi-panel): Comic art that is regularly published, has a recurring cast of characters, and usually has multiple panels that tell a story or a joke.

comics: A popular term for comic art.

editorial or political cartoon: A cartoon that takes a position on politics or other social issues.

gag cartoon: A single-panel humorous cartoon.

panel: The enclosed space on the page in which comic artists create their work.

sequential art: A series of panels a comic artist uses to tell a story or express an idea; examples are comic strips, comic books, and graphic novels.

sequential artist: An artist who creates sequential art.

speech or thought balloon: The line around dialogue in comic art that lets the reader know who is speaking; it can also show who is thinking something.

For More Information

Books

Bill Blackbeard and Martin Williams, eds. *The Smithsonian Collection of Newspaper Comics.* Washington, DC: Smithsonian Institution, 1977. This book showcases the history of comic strips and includes reprints of the greatest comic strips.

John Carlin, Paul Karasik, and Brian Walker, eds. *Masters of American Comics.* New Haven, CT: Yale University Press, 2005. This book focuses on fifteen comic artists and discusses the artistry they helped develop in comic art.

Les Daniels. *DC Comics: A Celebration of the World's Favorite Comic Book Heroes.* New York: Billboard, 2003. This history of DC Comics heroes like Superman and Batman has great pictures and a real inside look at how artists developed them.

Les Daniels. *Marvel: Five Decades of the World's Greatest Comics.* New York: Abrams, 1991. An interesting history of Marvel Comics, whose characters include Captain America and Spider-Man.

Will Eisner. *Comics and Sequential Art.* Tamarac, FL: Poorhouse, 1985. This celebrated comic artist explains techniques to create comic strips and comic books.

Jules Feiffer. *The Great Comic Book Heroes.* Seattle: Fantagraphics, 2003. This renowned comic artist discusses comic book heroes and the artists who drew them.

Ron Goulart. *The Great Comic Book Artists.* New York: St. Martin's, 1986. This book on comic book artists provides interesting details on their art and their lives.

Ron Goulart. *Ron Goulart's Great History of Comic Books.* Chicago: Contemporary Books, 1986. An interesting book on how comic books developed.

Robert C. Harvey. *The Art of the Comic Book: An Aesthetic History.* Jackson: University Press of Mississippi, 1996. Harvey details how the artistry of comic books developed by discussing top comic books and comic book artists.

Robert C. Harvey. *Children of the Yellow Kid*. Seattle: Frye Art Museum, 1998. An excellent book on comic strips that explains how the artistry of the best comic strip artists developed.

Syd Hoff. *Editorial and Political Cartooning*. New York: Stravon Educational Press, 1976. This celebrated cartoonist discusses the art of editorial cartoons as well as the impact they have had on history.

Gerard Jones. *Men of Tomorrow: Geeks, Gangsters and the Birth of the Comic Book*. New York: Basic Books, 2004. The author discusses how adventure comic strips like Dick Tracy helped lead to the development of comic books.

Richard Marschall. *America's Great Comic-Strip Artists: From the Yellow Kid to Peanuts*. New York: Stewart, Tabori and Chang, 1997. The author uses examples of famous comic strips to explain how comic strip art developed.

Roger Sabin. *Comics, Comix and Graphic Novels: A History of Comic Art*. London: Phaidon, 1996. An interesting look at the development of comic art in both the United States and Great Britain.

Brian Walker. *The Comics: The Complete Collection*. New York: Abrams, 2008. This comic artist and son of famed artist Mort Walker explains the development of comic strips.

Periodicals

John Benson. "Will Eisner: Having Something to Say." *Comics Journal*, February 2, 2011. www.tcj.com/will-eisner-having-something-to-say.

Gary Groth. "Jack Kirby Interview." *Comics Journal*, May 23, 2011. www.tcj.com/jack-kirby-interview.

Chris Mautner. "'It's Only One Book': An Art Spiegelman Interview." *Comics Journal*, November 17, 2011. www.tcj.com/an-art-spiegelman-interview.

Websites

Cartoon America: A Library of Congress Exhibition (www.loc.gov/exhibits/cartoonamerica/cartoonamerica-home.html.) A collection of historic cartoons.

Comic Art and Graffix Gallery (www.comic-art.com/history.htm). The site features a history of comic art, explained by pictures and narrative.

Comic Book Resources (www.comicbookresources.com). News, reviews, blogs, and articles about current comic books.

Comic Timeline: The History of the Funnies in America (www.infoplease.com/spot/comicstimeline.html). An interactive time line on the development of comic art, with interesting graphics.

GoComics (www.gocomics.com). This site has links to numerous comic strips and cartoons.

Integrative Arts 10 (www.psu.edu/dept /inart10_110/inart10/strip.html). This Pennsylvania State University site traces the history of comic and sequential art.

Herblock's History: Political Cartoons from the Crash to the Millennium (www.loc.gov/rr/print/swa nn/herblock). This Library of Congress site has a collection of historic editorial cartoons by Herb Block.

History of Comic Books (www.the comicbooks.com/old/frames.html). This site traces the history of comic books and includes biographies of several well-known comic artists.

ImageTexT Interdisciplinary Comics Studies (www.english.ufl.edu /imagetext). A University of Florida site dedicated to academic research on comic strips, comic books, and animated cartoons.

Stu's Comic Strip Connection (www .stus.com/3majors.htm). This site contains dozens of links to syndicated cartoon strips.

Index

Picture Credits

About the Author

Michael V. Uschan has written nearly ninety books, including *Life of an American Soldier in Iraq*, for which he won the 2005 Council for Wisconsin Writers Juvenile Nonfiction Award. It was the second time he won the award. Uschan began his career as a writer and editor with United Press International, a wire service that provides stories to newspapers, radio, and television. Journalism is sometimes called "history in a hurry," and Uschan considers writing history books a natural extension of the skills he developed in his many years as a journalist. He and his wife, Barbara, reside in the Milwaukee suburb of Franklin, Wisconsin.